SILVANA'S
GLUTEN-FREE *and* DAIRY-FREE
KITCHEN

SILVANA'S
GLUTEN-FREE *and* DAIRY-FREE
KITCHEN

Timeless Favorites
Transformed

SILVANA NARDONE

Photography by John Kernick

A RUX MARTIN BOOK

Houghton Mifflin Harcourt

Boston New York 2014

Copyright © 2014 by Silvana Nardone
Photographs © 2014 by John Kernick

For information about permission to reproduce selections from this book,
write to Permissions, Houghton Mifflin Harcourt Publishing Company,
215 Park Avenue South, New York, New York 10003.

www.hmhco.com

The recipe for My Gluten-Free All-Purpose Flour on page 195 initially
appeared as Silvana's All-Purpose Flour Blend in *Cooking for Isaiah:
Gluten-Free & Dairy-Free Recipes for Easy, Delicious Meals*, published
by Sprig, a division of Reader's Digest Association, Inc., © 2010. Used
with permission.

Library of Congress Cataloging-in-Publication Data.
Nardone, Silvana.
  Silvana's gluten-free & dairy-free kitchen : timeless favorites trans-
formed / Silvana Nardone ; photography by John Kernick.
     pages cm
  title: Silvana's gluten-free and dairy-free kitchen
  "A Rux Martin Book."
   ISBN 978-0-544-15734-7 (hardback); 978-0-544-16010-1 (ebk)
1. Gluten-free diet—Recipes. 2. Milk-free diet—Recipes. I. Kernick,
John, illustrator. II. Title. III. Title: Silvana's gluten-free and dairy-free
kitchen.
  RM237.86.N38 2014
  641.5'638—dc23

Book design by Kimberly Glyder

Printed in the United States of America
DOW 10 9 8 7 6 5 4 3 2 1

Food styling by Tracey Seaman

To my beautiful children,
Isaiah and Chiara, who have changed
me forever by inspiring me every
day to live our best lives.

CONTENTS

Hand-Rolled Bagels (page 55)

INTRODUCTION

Say Hello to Your New Gluten-Free Favorites

"My daughter Kelly and I still laugh about the first time I made your bread slabs. They were supposed to accompany dinner, but they wound up being dinner. We both just sat there slathering the warm bread with butter and laughing. They were the best things we had eaten in months!"
— *Betsy (California)*

"You have probably heard it a hundred times by now, but you have truly saved my family. Your cookbook and your blog have given me all the confidence in the world."
— *Kathy (Idaho)*

In the years since my first book—*Cooking for Isaiah: Gluten-Free & Dairy-Free Recipes for Easy, Delicious Meals*—launched, along with my blog, Silvana's Kitchen, I've been overwhelmed by the responses from moms across the country who have shared their personal stories and treasured family recipes by e-mail, blog comments, Facebook, Instagram and Twitter.

From the many food requests I've received, I've developed recipes for foods that families across America have missed because they are sensitive or allergic to gluten and dairy. Today we are all part of the new American family, where it's "normal" for at least one family member to have a food allergy or intolerance. Through endless testing, I've found a way to bring our favorite dishes back to the table—the foods that we used to eat at our favorite bakeries or restaurants, that we could just grab at the supermarket or that we made all the time at home.

If you think Classic Fluffy Pancakes are a thing of the past, think again. Need easy-to-slice Sandwich Loaf Bread or want toasted Hand-Rolled Bagels? They're here. For your next party, you'll find everything from Jalapeño Poppers, Crispy Chicken Taquitos and Cheesy Spinach-Artichoke Dip to Salted Soft Pretzel Poppers and even Deep-Dish Pizza Supreme. Do you long for Chinese food? My Crispy Shrimp and Pork Potstickers, Shrimp Fried Rice and Sweet-and-Sour Chicken will satisfy your cravings. And remember putting in your order every January for Thin Mints with your local Girl Scouts? My Thin Minty Cookies replicate that best-selling classic.

How did I do it? After years of running the test kitchen at *Every Day with Rachael Ray*, owning an Italian bakery and developing recipes for major magazines like *Food & Wine*, I've absorbed more than my share of culinary knowledge. Each experience has prepared me for the challenge of adapting recipes to make them gluten-free—without sacrificing texture or flavor. Sometimes, my recipes are even better than the original. And they will satisfy the toughest critics of all—your kids.

Duplicating flavors meant spending hours reading labels on packages at the supermarket and researching how ingredients—sometimes unknown to me—could improve texture. Ultimately, it involved testing and more testing in the kitchen—trying one thing after another until I finally got exactly what I was after and I had re-created that memory of the long-lost dish. For six years, breads were a particular challenge. In a moment of despair, I threw in every ingredient I thought would help create the physical characteristics of a beautifully baked loaf—baking powder, yeast and vitamin C—to give the dough its best chance to rise loftily. I was finally rewarded with lightness and an airy crumb.

I first joined the gluten-free community after my son, Isaiah, was diagnosed with gluten sensitivity. It took months for his doctors and me to figure out why he was constantly sick with colds, had an upset stomach, lacked energy and had dozens of warts on his hands and knees. To Discovering that eliminating gluten and dairy from his diet—something I could control—helped his health problems changed me forever. I learned that, like Isaiah, millions of Americans can't tolerate gluten or have celiac disease, an autoimmune digestive disease that damages the small intestines and prevents nutrient absorption.

For Isaiah, acidic foods like dairy further aggravated his intestinal lining, which was already raw from the gluten sensitivity. Getting rid of dairy meant a faster recovery. Re-creating his favorite foods without dairy proved to be quite the task. For solutions, I researched other diets and cooking techniques, including raw food and molecular gastronomy, which armed me with a bunch of useful ingredients and techniques and helped me develop my own version of dairy-free milk, yogurt, ricotta cheese and dulce de leche (see pages 204–223).

At the time of Isaiah's diagnosis, I couldn't have predicted the number of gluten- and dairy-free products that now line our supermarket shelves and freezer sections. Gluten-free options have even popped up in some local and chain restaurants. Ultimately, however, nothing beats the comfort of a home-cooked meal, and comfort means anything that my kids enjoyed before Isaiah's diagnosis.

So, how's Isaiah doing these days? I'm not a doctor, naturopath or nutritionist, but what I've seen with my own eyes continues to inspire me. He isn't plagued with colds and doesn't need to run to the bathroom anymore after eating school lunch. Then there's his energy. Thank goodness it's back. As a senior in high school who is now taller than I am, he needs all he can get.

To this day, it still astonishes me that with just a little knowledge, we can make dishes that have the power to help our bodies heal themselves.

Getting Started

Press the restart button on your diet and you'll feel the difference. Give yourself a break. When you or someone in your family is first diagnosed with gluten intolerance or celiac disease, it can be overwhelming. Go back to basics and eat naturally gluten-free foods you already know how to prepare. The list of what you can eat is endless. Stick to proteins, vegetables, fruits and starches like potatoes, rice and polenta.

Reclaim the rights to your favorite foods now. Start by removing all of the foods containing gluten and dairy. Then restock your cabinets, fridge and freezer (see below and page 4–6) so you have ingredients on hand that will make cooking and baking easier and faster. Once you're stocked up, all you have to do is make a weekly trip to the supermarket to round out your pantry with fresh ingredients like fruits and vegetables, meats and fish.

Spoil yourself and your family while making new food traditions. At first, you may wrestle with what it means to be a gluten-free family from every perspective—home life, siblings, school and birthday parties.

Yes, things will change, but it will bring your family closer and, as is the case with most truths, once you let your friends and children's teachers know, doors you never knew existed will open.

Choose the right ingredients to re-create the perfect flavor and texture in baked goods. Gluten-free or not, baking is a science, and ingredients are part of the formula. Through trial and error, you'll learn—just as I did—that some ingredients perform better than others, especially in gluten-free baking. Not all flour blends are created equal and not all flour blends can be substituted cup for cup for traditional all-purpose flour in recipes. My Gluten-Free All-Purpose Flour is comparable to unbleached all-purpose flour. A "healthier," high-protein flour blend—My Gluten-Free Sandwich Loaf Bread and Pizza Mix—is comparable to bread flour or whole wheat flour. Which you choose depends on what you're using it for. Brownies, for instance, are supposed to be a treat, not a power bar, so base your decision on expectations, dietary needs and health preferences.

Pantry Essentials

Depending on your experience, cooking without gluten and dairy may mean getting to know new ingredients that will make all the difference in your results.

Stock your cupboards and fridge with these three basics and you'll be ready to make family meals in no time.

1. My Gluten-Free All-Purpose Flour (page 195)
2. Liquid for browning and body: Homemade Cashew Milk or Almond Milk (page 205 or 206) or store-bought
3. Fat for texture and browning: Store-bought, nonhydrogenated, all-vegetable shortening

Key Ingredients

They can be found in health food stores and, more and more these days, in large supermarkets.

GLUTEN-FREE FLOURS
My go-to brand for all these flours is Bob's Red Mill, which is readily available in supermarkets across America and online.

White rice flour: This is the main ingredient in My Gluten-Free All-Purpose Flour (page 195). It is light, has a neutral flavor and blends easily with other gluten-free flours. It's made from rice (with the bran and germ removed) that has been ground into a fine, powdery flour.

Tapioca flour: This starch comes from cassava root. It's generally used as a thickening agent, but it's what has made all of the difference in My Gluten-Free All-Purpose Flour (page 195), giving the dough an elasticity that other popular gluten-free starches do not.

Potato starch: This starch made from potatoes has a low moisture content and gives baked goods a fluffy texture.

Millet flour: This buttery, slightly sweet flour is made from grinding millet seeds. It gives baked goods an almost cakey texture.

Sorghum flour: Milled from the sorghum grain, this flour is higher in protein than most gluten-free flours and has a mild, almost whole wheat–like flavor, making it a good choice for breads.

Sweet white rice flour: This flour is made from milling a short-grain rice, which, when cooked, is known for its sticky qualities. In some recipes, these highly starchy and binding qualities add stretchiness to the dough.

GLUTEN-FREE DOUGH ENHANCERS
Xanthan gum: This plant-based emulsifier, thickener and binder is made by fermenting a carbohydrate and creating a gel, which is then dried and milled into a fine powder. Xanthan gum gives foods body and structure, and it also provides a creamy texture. In dough, it provides elasticity and viscosity.

Golden flaxseed meal: Made from finely milled golden flaxseeds, this highly nutritious ingredient has gelling properties. I use it as a binder in breads, as I would use eggs, and to boost nutritional value.

Raw organic rice protein powder: This easily digestible powder that comes from brown rice replaces the protein found in high-protein bread flours. A higher protein content yields the highest-rising yeasted bread loaves and results in the chewiest of pizza crusts.

Psyllium husk powder: Psyllium is the husk of the plantain seed and contains a spongy fiber that soaks up liquid in a dough. I prefer psyllium in its powder form, which absorbs liquid faster than the husks. I use it in bread recipes because it makes the dough easy to handle and shape. It also contributes to the springy crumb of the baked bread.

Vitamin C powder: Otherwise known as ascorbic acid, this not only gives a lift to yeasted dough, but also produces a faster rise by amplifying yeast growth.

Probiotics powder: Similar to sourdough, probiotics culture bread dough, not only making it more digestible, but also adding a slight tang. The same is true for Dairy-Free Traditional Yogurt (page 213).

Iota carrageenan: A natural powder that is extracted from red algae, this is used to produce gels with a soft, elastic texture. When you add the right ratio of iota carrageenan to dairy-free milk, you get a thick, light and stable yogurt.

Dairy-free yogurt culture starter: This blend of lactic acid bacteria helps culture dairy-free milk, yielding a characteristically mild sourness with a smooth, creamy texture.

Agave nectar: This neutrally flavored, low-glycemic and quick-dissolving syrup is made from agave plant varieties. It's 25 percent sweeter than sugar, so a little goes a long way. I use it to mimic the natural lactose sugars found in milk.

Brown rice syrup: Also called rice malt, this sweetener is produced by culturing cooked brown rice with enzymes to break down the starches, then straining the mixture and cooking the remaining liquid until it is reduced to a viscous consistency. I use it in place of light or dark corn syrup.

Miscellaneous

Almond butter: This is made by processing almonds (blanched or with skins on, roasted or raw) until crunchy or smooth. I often use it in place of peanut butter.

Goji berries: Similar in taste to dried cranberries, this superfood is one of the most nutritionally rich fruits on the planet.

Gluten-free chickpea miso: This paste is made from naturally fermented chickpeas that deliver flavor, along with vital probiotic bacteria.

Gluten-free oats: Because of possible cross contamination with wheat in the fields, use certified gluten-free oats.

Gluten-free hot dogs: Check ingredient labels to make sure there are no fillers containing gluten.

Powdered egg whites: This convenience product is useful for making royal icing. I also use it for Devil's Food Cookies (page 156).

Nut milk bag: After processing raw nuts in a high-speed blender, I use a fine-mesh nylon nut milk bag to strain the milk from the pulp.

My Favorite Store-Bought Gluten-Free and Dairy-Free Products

There are many competing brands on the market for store-bought gluten-free and dairy-free products. Here are the products I use regularly in my kitchen.

Bread

Udi's Gluten Free Whole Grain Bread

Udi's Gluten Free Pizza Crusts

Udi's Gluten Free Plain Tortillas

Canyon Bakehouse San Juan 7-Grain
    Gluten Free Bread

Canyon Bakehouse Deli Rye Style Gluten
    Free Bread

Pasta

Jovial Brown Rice Penne Rigate

Jovial Brown Rice Tagliatelle

Jovial Brown Rice Lasagna

DeBoles Corn Elbow Style Pasta

Cheese

Daiya Plain Cream Cheese Style Spread

Daiya Mozzarella Style Shreds

Daiya Cheddar Style Shreds

Daiya Cheddar Style Slices

Daiya Cheddar Style Wedges

Milk, Creamer and Yogurt

Califia Farms Unsweetened Pure Almond Milk

Califia Farms Unsweetened Coconut
    Almond Milk

So Delicious Original Coconut Milk Creamer

So Delicious Unsweetened Cashew Milk

So Delicious Plain Cultured Coconut
    Milk (yogurt)

So Delicious Plain Greek Style Cultured
    Coconut Milk (yogurt)

Spreads and Oils

Earth Balance Organic Whipped Natural
    Buttery Spread

Spectrum Non-Hydrogenated Organic
    Expeller Pressed Palm Oil Shortening

Spectrum High Heat Expeller Pressed
    Canola Spray Oil

Spectrum Organic Expeller Pressed
    Canola Oil

Salted Soft Pretzel Poppers (page 62)

Breakfast and Brunch

THE BREAKFAST CLUB

By far the most requested recipes from readers are for basics like golden waffles and blueberry muffins. That's undoubtedly because a simple stack of fluffy pancakes matters more than ever when you can't eat gluten. These tried-and-true classics will help you reclaim your childhood and continue breakfast traditions with your own family.

CLASSIC FLUFFY PANCAKES

My most requested recipe by far is for plain pancakes. I avoided them at first for one simple reason—it wasn't easy to make them taste good. My initial attempts were flat, not fluffy, and they looked uncooked on the inside. I figured I could maybe learn a thing or two from Bisquick, so I studied the ingredient list and built my knockoff blend without any of the additives. The little bits of fat from the flecks of shortening throughout the pancake mix make lovely pockets that result in puffy, light pancakes.

Makes: Sixteen 3-inch pancakes   **Prep Time: 5 minutes**   **Cook Time: 16 minutes**

2 cups My Gluten-Free Pancake, Waffle and Biscuit Mix (page 196)

1⅓ cups Homemade Cashew or Almond Milk (page 205 or 206) or store-bought

2 large eggs, at room temperature

2 teaspoons pure vanilla extract

Canola oil, for greasing

Pure maple syrup, for serving

1. In a medium bowl, whisk together the pancake mix, milk, eggs and vanilla to combine.

2. Heat a large nonstick pan over medium heat. Using a paper towel, lightly grease with oil. Working in batches, pour the batter, about ¼ cup at a time, onto the pan and cook until golden, about 2 minutes on each side. (*The pancakes can be kept warm in a 200°F oven for up to 15 minutes.*) Serve with maple syrup.

VARIATIONS

CLASSIC BLUEBERRY PANCAKES: Just before cooking, stir fresh or frozen (not defrosted) blueberries into the batter.

WHOLE-GRAIN PANCAKES: Swap sorghum flour, millet flour, cornmeal or gluten-free rolled oats (or a combination) for half of the pancake mix.

SILVER DOLLAR PANCAKES: Portion out 1 tablespoon of the batter for each pancake.

BUTTERMILK PANCAKES: Use Dairy-Free Buttermilk (page 207) instead of the cashew or almond milk.

CINNAMON SWIRL PANCAKES WITH MAPLE ICING

Before I conquered yeasted cinnamon buns (page 50), I made these pancakes to satisfy that craving. They actually resemble the buns, too, down to their cinnamon swirl and sugary icing. Things go much faster if you have the cinnamon swirl mixture prepared ahead of time.

Makes: **Fifteen 3-inch pancakes**　　Prep Time: **12 minutes**　　Cook Time: **15 minutes**

FOR THE CINNAMON SWIRL FILLING

- ½ cup shortening, at room temperature
- 1 cup packed light brown sugar
- 1 tablespoon ground cinnamon

FOR THE ICING

- 1 cup confectioners' sugar, sifted
- 3 tablespoons pure maple syrup
- 1 tablespoon water

FOR THE PANCAKES

- 2 cups My Gluten-Free Pancake, Waffle and Biscuit Mix (page 196)
- 1½ cups Homemade Cashew or Almond Milk (page 205 or 206) or store-bought
- 2 large eggs, at room temperature
- 2 teaspoons pure vanilla extract
- Canola oil, for greasing

1. **Make the cinnamon swirl filling:** Place the shortening, brown sugar and cinnamon in a large resealable plastic bag and seal. Using your hands, mash together until combined. Snip off a corner to make a $\frac{1}{8}$-inch-wide hole.

2. **Make the icing:** In a small bowl, whisk together the confectioners' sugar, maple syrup and water.

3. **Make the pancakes:** Place the pancake mix in a large bowl. In a medium bowl, whisk together the milk, eggs and vanilla. Add to the pancake mix and stir to combine. Heat a large nonstick pan over medium heat. Using a paper towel, lightly grease with oil. Pour the batter about $\frac{1}{4}$ cup at a time onto the pan and squeeze the cinnamon sugar filling in a circular pattern to make a swirl. Cook until golden, about 2 minutes on each side. Between batches, clean your skillet by running it under hot water, dry, then lightly grease.

4. Drizzle the icing over the pancakes and serve hot.

MAPLE NUT GRANOLA CLUSTERS

I wanted to make those little granola clusters you find in cereal boxes—something we could snack on, pour milk over for cereal or sprinkle on top of ice cream. I grind the nuts in a food processor so they stick together when baked.

This recipe is super flexible. Throw in some chia seeds, coconut, dried fruit, cocoa powder (about 1 tablespoon), cinnamon (about ½ teaspoon), vanilla bean seeds or even lemon zest. Want to add more sweetness? Swap in orange or apple juice for the water. The granola is oat-free, and I prefer it this way. You won't miss the oats either.

Makes: **About 7 cups granola**　·　Prep Time: **7 minutes (plus soaking)**　·　Cook Time: **1 hour 15 minutes**

2 cups walnuts

2 cups almonds

2 cups pecans

1 cup pumpkin seeds

¾ cup pure maple syrup

½ cup applesauce

¼ cup water

¼ cup goji berries, soaked for 15 minutes and patted dry, or unsoaked raisins (optional)

½ teaspoon salt

1. Preheat the oven to 300°F with a rack in the middle. Line a baking sheet with parchment paper.
2. In a food processor or using a knife, process or chop the walnuts, almonds, pecans and pumpkin seeds until coarsely chopped. In a medium bowl, stir together the nuts and seeds with the maple syrup, applesauce, water, goji berries, if using, and salt.
3. Spread the mixture evenly on the baking sheet. Bake until golden and crisp, about 1 hour 15 minutes. *(The clusters will keep in an airtight container for up to 1 week.)*

DULCE DE LECHE COCONUT– CORN FLAKE CRISPIES

For days when I'm pressed for time, I like to have on hand these simple stir-and-bake breakfast treats packed with cereal, nuts, raisins and coconut—all of which give me the energy I need in the morning. I used to use condensed milk to hold all of the ingredients together, but Dairy-Free Dulce de Leche is even better.

Makes: **18 crispies**   Prep Time: **8 minutes**   Cook Time: **12 minutes**

2 cups crushed corn flakes

1 cup raisins

1 cup sliced almonds

¾ cup unsweetened shredded coconut

1 cup Dairy-Free Dulce de Leche (page 209)

1. Preheat the oven to 375°F with a rack in the middle. Line a baking sheet with parchment paper.

2. In a large bowl, combine all the ingredients. Using a 1½-inch ice cream scoop or a tablespoon, place mounds of the mixture about 1 inch apart on the baking sheet.

3. Bake until golden, about 12 minutes. Let cool completely on a wire rack before serving. (*The crispies will keep in an airtight container for up to 1 week.*)

APPLE AND GRANOLA YOGURT PARFAITS

Granola recipes typically use a vegetable (or nut) oil—but I left it out in favor of almond butter, which I heat with an equal amount of maple syrup, then toss with oats and nuts. All that's left to do is spread the granola on a baking sheet and bake at a low temperature until dry and crunchy.

Makes: 4 parfaits   Prep Time: **14 minutes**   Cook Time: **30 minutes**

FOR THE GRANOLA

- 2 cups gluten-free old-fashioned rolled oats
- ½ cup chopped almonds or walnuts
- ¼ cup pumpkin seeds
- ¼ cup sunflower seeds
- ¼ cup golden flaxseed meal
- 2 teaspoons ground cinnamon
- 1½ teaspoons ground ginger
- 1½ teaspoons ground allspice
- 1 teaspoon salt
- ⅓ cup pure maple syrup
- ⅓ cup well-stirred creamy almond butter

FOR THE PARFAITS

- 4 cups Dairy-Free Traditional Yogurt (page 213) or store-bought or double recipe Dairy-Free Instant Yogurt (page 212)
- 4 cups finely chopped apples (about 3)
- Honey or maple syrup, for drizzling

1. **Make the granola**: Preheat the oven to 325°F with a rack in the middle. Line a baking sheet with parchment paper.

2. In a large bowl, toss together the oats, almonds, pumpkin seeds, sunflower seeds, flaxseed meal, cinnamon, ginger, allspice and salt.

3. In a small saucepan over low heat, combine the maple syrup and almond butter. Add to the oat mixture and toss to coat. Spread out on the baking sheet and bake, stirring about every 15 minutes, until toasted and almost dry, about 30 minutes. *(The granola will keep in an airtight container for up to 1 month.)*

4. **Assemble the parfaits**: Fill four tall glasses or parfait bowls with half of the yogurt. Top each with some of the granola, ¾ cup of the apples, a little more granola, and a drizzle of honey. Top with the remaining yogurt and apples and another drizzle of honey.

BLUEBERRY SWIRL MUFFINS

Between the whole blueberries and the blueberry swirl, these muffins deliver a burst of flavor in every bite. The lemon sugar makes the tops extra crunchy.

Makes: **12 muffins**   Prep Time: **20 minutes**   Cook Time: **25 minutes**

1¼ cups plus 1 teaspoon sugar

Finely grated zest of 1 lemon

2 cups fresh blueberries

2¼ cups My Gluten-Free All-Purpose Flour (page 195)

1 tablespoon baking powder

1 teaspoon salt

2 large eggs, at room temperature

½ cup canola oil

1 cup Homemade Cashew or Almond Milk (page 205 or 206) or store-bought

2 teaspoons pure vanilla extract

1. In a small bowl, stir together ¼ cup of the sugar and the lemon zest. Set aside.

2. Preheat the oven to 425°F with a rack in the middle. Spray a 12-cup muffin pan with cooking spray.

3. In a small saucepan over medium heat, bring 1 cup of the blueberries and 1 teaspoon of the sugar to a simmer. Cook, mashing occasionally, until thickened, about 5 minutes. Let cool to room temperature, about 10 minutes.

4. In a large bowl, whisk together the flour, baking powder and salt. In a medium bowl, beat together the remaining 1 cup sugar, eggs, oil, milk and vanilla until smooth. Add to the flour mixture and stir until just combined. Fold in the remaining 1 cup blueberries. Pour the batter into each prepared muffin pan cup until two-thirds full. Spoon about 1 teaspoon of the blueberry compote into each muffin batter center and, using a fork, swirl. Sprinkle generously with the lemon sugar. Bake until a toothpick inserted in the center comes out clean, 16 to 18 minutes. Let cool on a rack before serving. *(The muffins can be frozen in an airtight container for up to 1 month.)*

COCOA-CINNAMON COBBLESTONE MUFFINS

These muffins remind me of one of my favorite desserts—bread pudding—except that they're far more yeasty and not eggy at all. I leave the dough unsweetened and instead toss the dough balls in a cocoa-cinnamon sugar, which gives them just enough sweetness. The muffins are best eaten fresh from the oven.

Makes: **12 muffins**   Prep Time: **25 minutes**   Cook Time: **20 minutes**

FOR THE COCOA-CINNAMON SUGAR

- ¾ cup granulated sugar
- ¼ cup packed light brown sugar
- 1 tablespoon ground cinnamon
- 2 teaspoons cocoa powder

FOR THE DOUGH

- 1 recipe My Gluten-Free Sandwich Loaf Bread and Pizza Mix (page 197)
- 1 cup lukewarm water
- ½ cup Homemade Cashew or Almond Milk (page 205 or 206) or store-bought
- 2 large eggs, at room temperature
- 2 tablespoons canola oil
- ¼ cup shortening, melted
- 2 ounces dairy-free semisweet chocolate, melted, for drizzling

1. Line a 12-cup muffin pan with liners.
2. **Make the cocoa-cinnamon sugar:** In a small bowl, stir together all the ingredients.
3. **Make the dough:** Place the flour in the bowl of a stand mixer. Using the paddle attachment and with the motor on low speed, add the water, milk, eggs and oil and beat until combined. Increase the speed to medium and beat for 3 minutes.
4. Tear off about 1 tablespoon of dough, forming a ball. Dip in the melted shortening and roll in the cocoa-cinnamon sugar to coat. Repeat with the remaining dough, filling each muffin liner with about 3 dough balls. Cover the muffin pan loosely with plastic wrap and let rise at room temperature until doubled in size, about 1 hour.
5. Preheat the oven to 425°F with a rack in the middle.
6. Sprinkle the muffins generously with the remaining sugar mixture. Bake until puffed and golden, about 20 minutes. Drizzle with the melted chocolate. Serve warm.

BAKED APPLE-CINNAMON OATMEAL CUPS

My go-to flavor of store-bought instant oatmeal was apple-cinnamon. Instead of baking the oatmeal in a large pan, I prefer to make individual cups so that it isn't mushy and the edges get nicely caramelized. You can stir in ½ cup of your favorite nuts or swap in other dried fruit for the dried apples.

Makes: **10 oatmeal cups**   Prep Time: **5 minutes**   Cook Time: **30 minutes**

2½ cups gluten-free old-fashioned rolled oats

1 cup chopped dried apples

½ cup packed brown sugar

1 tablespoon ground cinnamon

1½ teaspoons baking powder

1 teaspoon salt

1½ cups Homemade Cashew or Almond Milk (page 205 or 206) or store-bought

½ cup unsweetened applesauce

1 large egg, at room temperature, lightly beaten

2 tablespoons canola oil

2 teaspoons pure vanilla extract

Granulated sugar, for sprinkling

Pure maple syrup, warmed, for serving (optional)

1. Preheat the oven to 375°F with a rack in the middle. Generously spray 10 cups of a 12-cup muffin pan with cooking spray.

2. In a large bowl, stir together the oats, apples, brown sugar, cinnamon, baking powder and salt.

3. In a medium bowl, whisk together the milk, applesauce, egg, oil and vanilla until combined. Pour over the oats mixture and stir to combine.

4. Divide evenly among the prepared muffin cups and sprinkle generously with granulated sugar. Bake until golden, 25 to 30 minutes. Let cool in the muffin pan for 5 minutes, then remove the oatmeal cups and let cool on a wire rack. To serve, drizzle with warm maple syrup, if using.

CINNAMON CRUNCH FRENCH TOAST STICKS

Homemade frozen French toast sticks are great to have on hand when you're rushing to get the kids off to school in the morning. I wanted to make sure they wouldn't be soggy. My solution: rice cereal. Before adding the egg-dipped bread to the hot skillet, I coat the sticks in a crunchy blend of crushed cereal, sugar and cinnamon, which gives the French toast its signature caramelized crust.

Serves: **4**   Prep Time: **10 minutes**   Cook Time: **15 minutes**

½ cup sugar

¼ cup finely crushed gluten-free rice cereal, such as Erewhon

2 teaspoons ground cinnamon

¼ teaspoon salt

½ cup Homemade Cashew or Almond Milk (page 205 or 206) or store-bought

2 large eggs

2 teaspoons pure vanilla extract

2 tablespoons canola oil, plus more as needed

8 slices Sandwich Loaf Bread (page 40) or store-bought gluten-free bread, crusts removed and cut into sticks

Pure maple syrup, for serving

1. In a small bowl, mix together the sugar, cereal crumbs, cinnamon and salt.

2. In a shallow bowl, whisk together the milk, eggs and vanilla.

3. Heat a large skillet over medium heat, add the oil and heat until slowly bubbling. Working in batches, dip the bread sticks in the egg mixture to coat, then dip one side of each stick into the cereal mixture. Add them to the skillet, cereal side down, and cook until a golden brown crust forms, 3 to 5 minutes. Sprinkle the tops generously with the cereal mixture, flip and cook for 2 minutes more. Keep the finished French toast sticks warm in a 250°F oven for up to 15 minutes. Repeat with the remaining sticks, adding more oil as needed. Serve with maple syrup. (*You can make a double batch of these and freeze for up to 1 month. To reheat, place the sticks on a wire rack and toast in a toaster oven at 400°F or on a medium setting, turning once, until golden and crunchy, about 10 minutes total.*)

VARIATION

CINNAMON EGGNOG FRENCH TOAST STICKS: For the holidays, swap in store-bought dairy-free eggnog for the milk.

RASPBERRY-NUT BREAKFAST BARS

I've been making versions of these breakfast bars for decades. Instead of using almond flour, I grind almonds in a food processor fine enough so they add moisture to the dough base, yet coarse enough so some crunchy almond pieces remain.

Makes: **16 bars**   Prep Time: **10 minutes**   Cook Time: **45 minutes**

1¼ cups My Gluten-Free All-Purpose Flour (page 195)

1 cup blanched slivered or sliced almonds, plus more for topping

½ cup sugar

1 teaspoon baking powder

½ teaspoon baking soda

½ teaspoon salt

½ cup cold shortening, cut into pieces

1 large egg

1 teaspoon pure vanilla extract

¾ cup raspberry jam

1. Preheat the oven to 350°F with a rack in the middle. Line a 9-inch square baking pan with a 12-inch-long sheet of foil or parchment.

2. Place the flour, almonds, sugar, baking powder, baking soda and salt in a food processor and process until the nuts are finely ground. Add the shortening and pulse until coarse crumbs form. Beat together the egg and vanilla, drizzle over the dough mixture and pulse until coarse crumbs form.

3. Transfer two thirds of the dough to the pan and press into the bottom to form an even layer. Spread the jam on top. Dot with the remaining dough in clumps and top with additional almonds. Bake until golden brown, 40 to 45 minutes. Let cool for at least 1 hour on a wire rack. Cut into squares and serve. *(The bars will keep in an airtight container for up to 1 week.)*

VARIATION

Use your favorite preserve in place of the raspberry jam. I love to use apricot or fig jam or even apple or pumpkin butter.

BANANA-CHOCOLATE OAT COOKIES

These nutrition-packed breakfast cookies are egg-free, but the combination of bananas, flaxseed and peanut butter binds the dough together, and the snacks are perfect for grab-and-go breakfasts.

Makes: **12 cookies** • Prep Time: **12 minutes** • Cook Time: **20 minutes**

1 cup gluten-free old-fashioned rolled oats

1 cup My Gluten-Free All-Purpose Flour (page 195)

2 tablespoons golden flaxseed meal

1 teaspoon baking powder

½ teaspoon ground cinnamon

1 medium ripe banana, mashed (about ½ cup)

½ cup packed brown sugar

⅓ cup vegetable oil

2 tablespoons Homemade Cashew or Almond Milk (page 205 or 206) or store-bought

2 tablespoons peanut butter or well-stirred almond butter

1 tablespoon pure vanilla extract

¾ cup dairy-free semisweet chocolate chips

1. Preheat the oven to 350°F with a rack in the middle. Line a baking sheet with parchment paper.

2. In a small bowl, combine the oats, flour, flaxseed, baking powder and cinnamon.

3. In a large bowl, combine the banana, brown sugar, oil, milk, peanut butter and vanilla. Stir in the oat mixture until combined. Stir in the chocolate chips.

4. Using a 1½-inch scoop or a rounded tablespoon, drop the dough 2 inches apart onto the baking sheet and flatten gently. Bake until golden, 18 to 20 minutes. Let cool on a rack before serving. *(The cookies will keep in an airtight container for up to 1 week.)*

CLASSIC SWEET WAFFLES

I grew up eating frozen Eggo Homestyle Waffles. I loved the sweet smell in the air as they toasted almost as much as I did their crispy edges and cakey insides. By calibrating this waffle batter so it wasn't too thick or watery, I was able to get just the right texture. A double dose of vanilla extract gives the waffles their classic flavor.

Serves: **4**   Prep Time: **5 minutes**   Cook Time: **16 minutes**

2 cups My Gluten-Free Pancake, Waffle and Biscuit Mix (page 196)

1⅓ cups Homemade Cashew or Almond Milk (page 205 or 206) or store-bought

2 large eggs, at room temperature, lightly beaten

2 teaspoons pure vanilla extract

Pure maple syrup, for serving

1. Preheat a waffle iron to medium-high.
2. In a medium bowl, whisk together the pancake mix, milk, eggs and vanilla to combine.
3. Spray the waffle iron with nonstick cooking spray.
4. Pour a heaping ⅓ cup batter into each waffle iron square. Close and cook until crisp, about 4 minutes. Repeat with the remaining batter. Serve with syrup. (*The waffles can be frozen in an airtight container for up to 1 month.*)

VARIATION

CLASSIC SAVORY WAFFLES: In my first days of going gluten-free, savory waffles were my sandwich salvation. Especially when I'm making waffles for sandwich use, I cook them in a square waffle iron to yield a size that pairs perfectly with a slice of dairy-free cheese.

You can stir up to a ½ cup of mix-ins (such as cooked ham, bacon, sausage, salami, mushrooms, cooked spinach and any fresh or dried herbs) into the waffle batter before cooking.

Proceed as directed above but swap in 1 tablespoon Dijon mustard for the vanilla. Serve hot or let cool.

FLUFFY BUTTERMILK BISCUITS

I appreciate a fluffy, buttery biscuit. This recipe is my take on classic Bisquick biscuits with one seemingly minor addition: honey. I know that's the reason these biscuits always disappear shortly after they come out of the oven. They are best eaten the same day.

Makes: **Eight 2-inch biscuits** • Prep Time: **5 minutes** • Cook Time: **10 minutes**

2¼ cups My Gluten-Free Pancake, Waffle and Biscuit Mix (page 196)

½ teaspoon salt

¼ teaspoon baking soda

⅔ cup Dairy-Free Buttermilk (page 207) or Homemade Cashew or Almond Milk (page 205 or 206) or store-bought

1 tablespoon honey

1 large egg beaten with 1 tablespoon water, for egg wash

1. Preheat the oven to 450°F with a rack in the middle. Line a baking sheet with parchment paper.
2. In a large bowl, whisk together the pancake mix, salt and baking soda. Stir in the buttermilk and honey until a dough forms.
3. Place the dough on a piece of parchment paper and roll out until about ¾ inch thick. Cut the dough with a 2-inch round cutter and place the rounds about 2 inches apart on the baking sheet. Brush with some of the egg wash.
4. Bake until puffed and golden, 8 to 10 minutes. Serve warm or let cool on a wire rack.

ORANGE MARMALADE–STREUSEL SCONES

Millet flour doesn't alter the color or texture of a baked good and adds a wonderfully warming, almost buttery flavor. I use a ratio of one third millet flour here, but you can swap in up to ³/₄ cup millet flour. If you don't have millet flour on hand, substitute an equal amount of My Gluten-Free All-Purpose Flour (page 195).

Makes: **8 scones**   Prep Time: **14 minutes (plus chilling)**   Cook Time: **30 minutes**

FOR THE STREUSEL

- ¼ cup My Gluten-Free All-Purpose Flour (page 195)
- ¼ cup sugar
- 2 tablespoons finely chopped walnuts
- 2 tablespoons shortening, softened
- 1 tablespoon finely grated lemon zest

FOR THE SCONES

- 1¼ cups homemade dairy-free heavy cream (page 205) or store-bought dairy-free creamer, plus more for brushing
- 1 teaspoon apple cider vinegar
- 1½ cups My Gluten-Free All-Purpose Flour (page 195)
- ½ cup millet flour
- 2 tablespoons sugar
- 1 tablespoon baking powder
- ½ teaspoon salt
- 6 tablespoons shortening, frozen and cut into ¼-inch pieces
- 1 large egg, lightly beaten
- ½ cup orange marmalade

1. Preheat the oven to 350°F with a rack in the middle. Line a baking sheet with parchment paper.

2. **Make the streusel:** In a small bowl, mix together all the ingredients until coarse crumbs form.

3. **Make the scones:** In a small bowl, stir together the cream and vinegar.

4. In a large bowl, whisk together the all-purpose flour, millet flour, sugar, baking powder and salt. Cut in the shortening with a fork or fingers until coarse crumbs form. Add the cream mixture and the egg; stir with a fork to combine.

5. Divide the dough into 2 pieces and shape each into a ³/₄-inch-thick circle. Cover 1 circle with the marmalade. Top with the other circle and press down gently. Cut into 8 triangles.

6. Place triangles about 2 inches apart on the baking sheet and refrigerate for 30 minutes. Brush with cream and top with the streusel. Bake until golden, about 30 minutes. Serve. *(The scones will keep in an airtight container for up to 3 days.)*

FRIED CINNAMON-SUGAR BISCUIT BITES

Frying gives these biscuits a delicious crunchiness on the outside and a light fluffiness inside. After frying, I toss the biscuits in cinnamon sugar.

Makes: **24 bites**   Prep Time: **10 minutes**   Cook Time: **25 minutes**

Vegetable oil, for frying

½ cup plus 2 tablespoons sugar

2 teaspoons ground cinnamon

Finely grated zest of 1 orange

Salt

2 cups My Gluten-Free All-Purpose Flour (page 195), plus more for dusting

1 tablespoon baking powder

½ cup shortening, frozen and cut into ¼-inch pieces

¾ cup homeade dairy-free heavy cream (page 205) or store-bought dairy-free creamer

1 large egg, lightly beaten

1 tablespoon pure vanilla extract

1. Fill a large pot with about 2 inches of oil and heat over medium-high heat until it registers 365°F on a deep-fat thermometer.
2. Meanwhile, in a small bowl, stir together ½ cup of the sugar, the cinnamon, zest and ¼ teaspoon salt. Set the cinnamon sugar aside.
3. In a large bowl, whisk together the flour, remaining 2 tablespoons sugar, baking powder and ¾ teaspoon salt. Cut in the shortening with a fork or fingers until coarse crumbs form. Stir in the creamer, egg and vanilla with a fork; stir to combine.
4. Working in batches of about 4, spoon about 2 tablespoons of the dough and carefully lower into the hot oil. Fry the biscuits, turning occasionally, until golden brown and cooked through, about 4 minutes. Remove with a slotted spoon and drain on paper towels. Dredge the warm biscuit bites in the cinnamon sugar to coat and serve.

VARIATION

BAKED CINNAMON-SUGAR BISCUIT BITES: To bake, preheat the oven to 350°F with a rack in the middle. Line a baking sheet with parchment paper and using a ¼-cup ice cream scoop, drop the dough into the cinnamon-sugar mixture and turn to coat, then place on the baking sheet. Bake until golden and puffed, about 30 minutes. Let cool on a wire rack. (*The uncooked coated biscuits can be frozen in a single layer, then placed in a resealable freezer bag for up to 1 month. Thaw before baking.*)

MUESLI FLATBREAD ROUNDS

These flatbreads are perfect for breakfast on the go. Just toast and spread with your favorite jam, nut butter or Dairy-Free Ricotta Cheese (page 215).

Makes: 12 flatbreads   **Prep Time: 14 minutes (plus rising)**   **Cook Time: 9 minutes**

1   recipe My Gluten-Free Sandwich Loaf Bread and Pizza Mix (page 197)

2   tablespoons millet flour

¼   cup gluten-free old-fashioned rolled oats

¼   cup golden raisins

¼   cup chopped dried apples

1   tablespoon sugar

1½ teaspoons salt

1½ cups lukewarm water

2   tablespoons canola oil

1   large egg, at room temperature

1. In a large bowl, whisk together the bread flour, millet flour, oats, raisins, apples, sugar and salt. Add the water, oil and egg and stir together until combined. Let sit for 7 minutes until thickened.

2. On a clean, lightly floured surface, knead the dough until smooth and elastic, about 1 minute. Divide the dough into 12 equal pieces and, using a rolling pin, loosely shape each into a circle about ¼ inch thick. Cover with plastic wrap and let sit at room temperature until puffy, about 1 hour.

3. Heat a dry cast-iron skillet over medium heat. Working in batches of 4, place the dough in the hot pan and cook, turning once, until puffy, about 3 minutes. Transfer to a baking sheet and repeat with the remaining dough. Serve at room temperature. (*The rounds will keep in an airtight container between sheets of parchment for up to 3 days. Toast to warm.*)

SCRAMBLED EGG, POTATO AND SPINACH BREAKFAST TACOS

When I was in Austin, Texas, I visited Magnolia Cafe and had the best breakfast taco ever. At home, I came up with my own version. The doubled-up corn tortillas prevent the tacos from collapsing. To warm the tortillas until pliable, wrap them in foil and warm in a 350°F oven until heated through, 10 to 15 minutes. Or, heat them, stacked, in the microwave on high for 30 seconds. Or, char them slightly in a hot cast-iron skillet.

Makes: 4 tacos   Prep Time: **15 minutes**   Cook Time: **15 minutes**

1 large Yukon Gold potato, cut into ½-inch pieces

2 tablespoons canola oil

2 garlic cloves, smashed

1 5-ounce bag baby spinach

Salt and black pepper

6 large eggs, at room temperature

2 tablespoons Homemade Cashew or Almond Milk (page 205 or 206) or store-bought

8 corn tortillas, warmed (see above)

¼ cup chopped fresh cilantro or parsley

Store-bought salsa, for serving

1. Place the potatoes in a small saucepan, add cold salted water to cover by 1 inch and bring to a boil over medium-high heat. Cook until fork-tender, about 10 minutes. Drain.

2. In a medium skillet, heat 1 tablespoon of the oil over medium heat and cook the garlic until golden. Add the spinach and ¼ teaspoon salt. Cook until wilted, about 1 minute. Transfer to a bowl, remove the garlic and clean the skillet.

3. Heat the remaining 1 tablespoon oil in the skillet over medium heat. In a small bowl, whisk together the eggs, milk, ½ teaspoon salt and ¼ teaspoon pepper. Add to the skillet and cook, stirring occasionally, until softly scrambled, about 3 minutes.

4. Divide the eggs, potatoes and spinach among warmed doubled-up corn tortillas, top with cilantro and salsa and serve.

BREAKFAST SAUSAGE–STUFFING CASSEROLE

This Thanksgiving brunch casserole has been a favorite of mine for years. It's a sweet-savory bread pudding with breakfast sausage, cranberries and walnuts. Sprinkling it with confectioners' sugar and drizzling it with maple syrup make it even more decadent.

Serves: **6**   Prep Time: **16 minutes**   Cook Time: **1 hour 10 minutes**

12 ounces gluten-free breakfast pork sausage meat

1 loaf sliced Sandwich Loaf Bread (page 40) or store-bought gluten-free bread, torn into pieces

1 cup dried cranberries

1 cup walnuts, toasted and coarsely chopped

1 teaspoon chopped fresh thyme

2 cups Homemade Cashew or Almond Milk (page 205 or 206) or store-bought

6 large eggs

2 tablespoons Dijon mustard

1½ teaspoons salt

¼ teaspoon black pepper

Confectioners' sugar, for dusting (optional)

Pure maple syrup, for serving (optional)

1. Preheat the oven to 350°F. Spray a 9-by-13-inch baking dish with cooking spray.

2. In a skillet over medium heat, cook the sausage, breaking it up with a wooden spoon, until browned, about 8 minutes. Drain and transfer to a large bowl. Add the bread pieces, cranberries, walnuts and thyme and toss. Transfer to the baking dish.

3. In a small bowl, whisk together the milk, eggs, mustard, 1½ teaspoons salt and ¼ teaspoon pepper. Pour over the stuffing in the dish and let sit for 5 minutes. (*The stuffing can be prepared up to 1 day ahead and refrigerated, covered. Bring to room temperature before baking.*)

4. Bake, uncovered, until a knife inserted into the center comes out clean, about 1 hour 10 minutes. Let stand for about 15 minutes before dusting with confectioners' sugar, if using. Serve with maple syrup, if using.

Breads and Flatbreads

These will be the most sought-after bunch of recipes on the block. The biggest issues with store-bought gluten-free bread are the taste and expense. After years of failures and small successes, I finally nailed the formula for gluten-free bread flour and created a loaf with the perfect rise and a more-than-satisfying chew. Now I can make sandwich bread, bagels or soft pretzels any day of the week.

I bake most of my breads in a cast-iron loaf pan, which ensures a crisp crust. If you substitute an ordinary loaf pan, the crust will not brown as much and will be softer.

PULL-APART ROLLS

Pull-apart rolls are one of my favorite Thanksgiving food traditions, and with my new bread blend, there's no reason you can't make them, too. I brush buttery spread over the dough before baking to give the finished rolls their golden hue and butter-like flavor. If you don't have buttery spread, just brush the rolls before baking with canola oil or olive oil.

Makes: **12 rolls**   Prep Time: **25 minutes (plus rising)**   Cook Time: **30 minutes**

1 recipe My Gluten-Free Sandwich Loaf Bread and Pizza Mix (page 197)

1½ cups lukewarm water

2 large eggs, at room temperature

2 tablespoons canola oil

¼ cup buttery spread, such as Earth Balance Organic Whipped, melted

1. Place the bread mix in the bowl of a stand mixer. Using the paddle attachment on low speed, add the lukewarm water, eggs and oil and mix until combined. Increase the speed to medium and beat the dough for 3 minutes.

2. On a lightly floured piece of parchment paper, roll the dough out into a rectangle about ½ inch thick. Using a pizza cutter, divide into 12 equal pieces. Transfer the dough with the parchment paper to a baking sheet, cover loosely with plastic wrap and let rise at room temperature until doubled in size, about 1 hour.

3. Preheat the oven to 375°F with a rack in the middle.

4. Brush the dough pieces generously with the melted buttery spread. Bake until puffed and golden, about 30 minutes. Let cool slightly, then transfer to a wire rack to cool before serving. *(The baked rolls can be stored in a sealed paper bag for up to 2 days or frozen in a resealable freezer bag for up to 1 month. Let thaw in the fridge the night before or at room temperature, then reheat in a 350°F oven until warm, about 10 minutes.)*

VARIATIONS

PULL-APART HERB ROLLS:
Replace ¼ cup of the bread mix with medium-grind cornmeal and add 1 teaspoon finely chopped thyme or rosemary.

PULL-APART BUTTERMILK ROLLS: Swap the water for homemade Dairy-Free Buttermilk (pg 207).

SANDWICH LOAF BREAD

It took me six years to get a sandwich bread to work. I can say with confidence that this is the ultimate everyday loaf—and it doesn't need to be toasted to taste wonderful. The outside has just the right amount of crust, while the inside crumb is soft and fluffy. Get ready to be surprised at how easy it is to make, too.

Makes: One 2-pound loaf   Prep Time: **15 minutes (plus rising)**   Cook Time: **1 hour 10 minutes**

1 recipe My Gluten-Free Sandwich Loaf Bread and Pizza Mix (page 197)

2 cups lukewarm water

2 large eggs, at room temperature

2 tablespoons canola oil

2 tablespoons melted shortening, for brushing (optional)

1. Place the bread mix in the bowl of a stand mixer. Using the paddle attachment on low speed, add the lukewarm water, eggs and oil and mix until combined. Increase the speed to medium and mix the dough for 3 minutes.

2. Transfer the dough to the loaf pan and, using an offset spatula, gently smooth out the surface. Cover loosely with plastic wrap and let rise at room temperature until the dough domes over the edge of the pan, about $1\frac{1}{2}$ hours.

3. About 20 minutes before baking, preheat the oven to 425°F with a rack in the middle. Spray a $10\frac{1}{4}$-by-$5\frac{1}{8}$-inch cast-iron loaf pan with cooking spray.

4. Bake the bread for 15 minutes. Reduce the heat to 350°F and bake for 50 to 55 minutes more, until the loaf is golden, sounds hollow when thumped on the bottom, and the internal temperature measures 208°F on an instant-read thermometer. Set on a wire rack and brush with the melted shortening, if using. Let cool before slicing. (*The cooled loaf can be stored in a sealed paper bag for up to 2 days or sliced and frozen in a resealable freezer bag for up to 1 month.*)

FRENCH BAGUETTES

I like to use sorghum flour for baguettes because it has a neutral yet sweet flavor. It also happens to be high in protein, which mimics regular bread flour. I recommend using baguette pans to help the loaves hold their shape. Their perforations allow for even heat distribution, which means even baking and browning.

If the loaves soften when cooled, just turn the oven back on and bake for another 5 to 10 minutes. The bread will get crusty—and stay that way.

Makes: Two 17-inch-long baguettes
Cook Time: 50 minutes

Prep Time: 10 minutes (plus rising and chilling)

2 cups My Gluten-Free All-Purpose Flour (page 195)

1 cup sorghum flour or millet flour

1 teaspoon xanthan gum

1½ teaspoons salt

1 ¼-ounce packet active dry yeast

2 large eggs, at room temperature

3 tablespoons olive oil

1 tablespoon honey

1½ cups lukewarm water

1. In the bowl of a stand mixer fitted with the paddle attachment on low speed, mix together the all-purpose flour, sorghum flour, xanthan gum, salt and yeast. Add the eggs, oil, honey and lukewarm water. With the motor on medium-high, mix for 4 minutes until a sticky, stretchy dough forms. Cover loosely with greased plastic wrap and let rise at room temperature for about 2 hours. Refrigerate for about 24 hours or up to 3 days.

2. About 20 minutes before baking, preheat the oven to 475°F with a rack in the middle.

3. Sprinkle flour over a sheet of parchment paper. Using wet hands, pull out half of the dough. Place on the parchment while gently lifting and stretching the dough into a baguette-like shape. Run warm water over your hands and gently smooth out the top and sides. Place the shaped dough with the parchment in a baguette pan and cover loosely with greased plastic wrap. Repeat with the remaining dough, putting it in the pan. Let rise at room temperature for about 1 hour, or until puffy.

4. Using a serrated knife, diagonally score the loaves 3 times, about ¼ inch deep. Bake for 20 minutes. Pull out the parchment paper and bake until the loaves are golden brown and sound hollow when thumped on the bottom and the internal temperature on an instant-read thermometer measures about 200°F, 20 to 30 minutes more.

5. Turn off the heat, open the oven door and let cool in the oven for 30 minutes. Place on a wire rack to cool completely before serving. *(The cooled loaves can be stored in a sealed paper bag for up to 2 days or frozen in a resealable freezer bag for up to 1 month.)*

RYE–SUNFLOWER SEED BREAD

I never thought I'd be eating rye bread again. I have Canyon Bakehouse's mock rye bread to thank for inspiring this remake. When I read through the ingredient list on the packaging, I realized that they used ground caraway seeds to give the dough that rye flavor without using high-gluten rye flour—genius! For this recipe, I prefer using a parchment paper cooking bag, which gives the bread its super-crusty exterior and soft interior. You can buy bags at kitchenware stores or on Amazon.

Makes: **2 small loaves**   Prep Time: **8 minutes (plus rising)**   Cook Time: **1 hour 25 minutes**

1 recipe My Gluten-Free Sandwich Loaf Bread and Pizza Mix (page 197)

⅓ cup sunflower seeds

3 tablespoons ground caraway seeds

2 teaspoons whole caraway seeds

1 teaspoon salt

1¾ cups lukewarm water

2 large eggs, at room temperature

2 tablespoons olive oil

My Gluten-Free All-Purpose Flour (page 195), for sprinkling

1. Place the bread mix in the bowl of a stand mixer. Using the paddle attachment on low speed, mix together the bread mix, sunflower seeds, ground and whole caraway seeds and salt. Add the lukewarm water, eggs and oil and mix until combined. Increase the speed to medium and beat the dough for 3 minutes.

2. Divide the dough into 2 equal pieces and place each on a piece of parchment paper. Using a wet offset spatula or a spoon, shape each piece of dough into a loaf shape and gently smooth out the surface. Cover each loosely with plastic wrap and let rise at room temperature for about 1½ hours.

3. About 20 minutes before baking, preheat the oven to 400°F with a rack in the middle.

4. Slide each piece of dough on the parchment into 8-by-3¼-by-14-inch parchment paper cooking bags, sprinkle the tops with flour and fold the bag opening several turns to seal. Place the cooking bags directly on the oven rack and bake until the loaves are crusty and sound hollow when thumped on the bottom, about 1 hour 25 minutes. Carefully tear open the bag (hot steam will escape) and let cool completely on a wire rack before serving. *(The cooled loaves can be stored in a sealed paper bag for up to 2 days or frozen in a resealable freezer bag for up to 1 month.)*

SEEDED OAT BROWN BREAD

The seeds provide a great nutrition boost and nice crunch. The apple cider vinegar acts as a dough enhancer, helping the dough to rise and giving the bread a crackly crust.

Makes: One 2-pound loaf   Prep Time: 15 minutes (plus rising)   Cook Time: 70 minutes

¼ cup sunflower seeds

¼ cup pumpkin seeds

¼ cup gluten-free steel-cut oats

2 tablespoons whole flaxseeds

2 tablespoons sesame seeds, plus more for sprinkling

1¾ cups lukewarm water

1 recipe My Gluten-Free Sandwich Loaf Bread and Pizza Mix (page 197)

2 large eggs, at room temperature

2 tablespoons canola oil

2 tablespoons molasses

1 teaspoon apple cider vinegar

1. In a small bowl, stir together the sunflower seeds, pumpkin seeds, oats, flaxseeds, sesame seeds and ¼ cup of the lukewarm water.

2. Place the bread mix in the bowl of a stand mixer. Using the paddle attachment on low speed, add the remaining 1½ cups lukewarm water, eggs, oil, molasses, vinegar and soaked-seed mixture until combined. Increase the speed to medium and beat the dough for 3 minutes.

3. About 20 minutes before baking, preheat the oven to 425°F with a rack in the middle. Spray a 10¼-by-5⅛-inch cast-iron loaf pan with cooking spray and sprinkle the sides with sesame seeds.

4. Transfer the dough to the loaf pan and, with an offset spatula, gently smooth out the surface. Cover loosely with plastic wrap and let rise at room temperature until the dough domes over the edge of the pan, about 1½ hours. Using a water spritzer, spray with warm water and sprinkle with more sesame seeds.

5. Bake for 15 minutes. Reduce the heat to 350°F, bake until the loaf is golden, sounds hollow when thumped on the bottom and the internal temperature measures 208°F, 50 to 55 minutes more. Let cool on a wire rack before serving. *(The cooled loaf can be stored in a sealed paper bag for up to 2 days or sliced and frozen in a resealable freezer bag for up to 1 month.)*

VARIATION

Add ¼ cup poppy seeds and ¾ cup dried mixed fruit to the seed mix.

CINNAMON-RAISIN BREAD

For a glossy finish, I usually brush the hot-out-of-the-oven loaf with simple syrup. Or, for a sugary cinnamon coating, I brush it with buttery spread or unflavored coconut oil and quickly roll it in a mixture of 2 tablespoons sugar and 2 teaspoons cinnamon. For a healthy touch, you can also scatter rice bran over the loaf before baking.

Makes: **One 2-pound loaf** ・ Prep Time: **14 minutes (plus rising)** ・ Cook Time: **1 hour 10 minutes**

1 recipe My Gluten-Free Sandwich Loaf Bread and Pizza Mix (page 197)

¼ cup packed light brown sugar

1 tablespoon ground cinnamon

1½ cups raisins

2 cups lukewarm water

2 large eggs, at room temperature

2 tablespoons canola oil

Sesame seeds, for sprinkling

FOR THE SIMPLE SYRUP

⅓ cup sugar

½ cup water

1. Place the bread mix in the bowl of a stand mixer. Using the paddle attachment on low speed, add the brown sugar and cinnamon and blend. Add the raisins and mix to coat. Add the lukewarm water, eggs and oil and mix to combine. Increase the speed to medium and mix the dough for 3 minutes.

2. Transfer the dough to the loaf pan and, using an offset spatula, gently smooth out the surface. Cover loosely with plastic wrap and let rise at room temperature until the dough domes over the edge of the pan, about 1½ hours.

3. About 20 minutes before baking, preheat the oven to 425°F with a rack in the middle. Spray a 10¼-by-5⅛-inch cast-iron loaf pan with cooking spray and sprinkle the sides with sesame seeds.

4. Bake for 15 minutes. Reduce the heat to 350°F and bake until the loaf is golden, sounds hollow when thumped on the bottom and the internal temperature on an instant-read thermometer measures 208°F, 50 to 55 minutes more. Let cool on a wire rack before serving.

5. **Meanwhile, make the simple syrup**: In a small saucepan, bring the sugar and water to a boil. Reduce the heat to medium and cook, stirring, until the sugar is dissolved, about 2 minutes.

6. Brush the syrup over the loaf. Let cool on a wire rack before serving. *(The cooled loaf can be stored in a sealed paper bag for up to 2 days or sliced or frozen in a resealable freezer bag for up to 1 month.)*

ICED CINNAMON BUNS

In high school, my older brother, Bernardo, worked at Cinnabon on weekends. When he returned from work, he walked into the house carrying the aroma on his clothes, filling the air with that sweetness of sugar and spice. Now I crave these sweet buns. Once I conquered the bread dough, I knew I was just moments away from success.

Makes: **16 buns**   Prep Time: **40 minutes (plus rising)**   Cook Time: **30 minutes**

FOR THE DOUGH

- 1 recipe My Gluten-Free Sandwich Loaf Bread and Pizza Mix (page 197)
- ¼ cup granulated sugar
- ¼ cup shortening, at room temperature
- 1 teaspoon salt
- ½ teaspoon ground nutmeg
- 2 large eggs, at room temperature
- 1¾ cups Homemade Cashew or Almond Milk (page 205 or 206) or store-bought, warmed
- 2 teaspoons pure vanilla extract

FOR THE FILLING

- 1 cup packed light brown sugar
- 1 tablespoon ground cinnamon
- ⅛ teaspoon salt
- 2 tablespoons shortening, melted

FOR THE ICING

- 3 cups confectioners' sugar
- ½ cup Homemade Cashew or Almond Milk (page 205 or 206) or store-bought, at room temperature
- 6 tablespoons shortening, melted
- ¼ teaspoon salt

1. **Make the dough:** In the bowl of a stand mixer fitted with a paddle attachment, mix together the bread mix, granulated sugar, shortening, salt and nutmeg on low speed. Add the eggs, milk and vanilla and mix until combined on medium speed.

2. **Make the filling:** In a medium bowl, combine the brown sugar, cinnamon, salt and melted shortening.

3. Spray two 9-inch metal pie pans with cooking spray. Roll out the dough to form a rectangle about ¼ inch thick. Scatter the filling over the dough, leaving about a ½-inch border. Beginning with the long edge nearest you, roll the dough up into a cylinder and place seam side down. Using a serrated knife, cut crosswise into 16 rolls. Place 8 rolls, cut side down, in a circular pattern in each prepared pan and cover with

plastic wrap. Let sit at room temperature until puffy, about 1 hour, or refrigerate overnight (let warm to room temperature before baking).

4. About 20 minutes before baking, preheat the oven to 375°F with a rack in the middle.

5. Bake the buns until puffed and golden, 25 to 30 minutes. Let cool on a wire rack for at least 10 minutes.

6. **Meanwhile, make the icing**: In a medium bowl, combine all the icing ingredients. Spread over the cooled rolls and serve.

ENGLISH MUFFINS

When I tried to make a gluten-free version of English muffins, I had my hands full trying to get those nooks and crannies just right. I ended up adding some oats and millet, which helped achieve the spot-on texture. I also substituted brown rice farina for the gluten-filled semolina farina in the Thomas' Original English Muffin recipe.

Makes: 12 English muffins   **Prep Time: 14 minutes (plus rising)**   **Cook Time: 50 minutes**

2 tablespoons whole millet

¼ cup boiling water

1 recipe My Gluten-Free Bagel and Pretzel Mix (page 198)

¼ cup gluten-free old-fashioned rolled oats

2 teaspoons sugar

1½ teaspoons salt

¾ teaspoon cream of tartar

½ teaspoon baking soda

1½ cups lukewarm water

¾ cup lukewarm milk

1 tablespoon canola oil

Brown rice farina or medium-grind cornmeal, for scattering

1. In a small bowl, combine the millet and boiling water. Let stand for 15 minutes, then drain.
2. In a large bowl, whisk together the bagel mix, oats, sugar, salt, cream of tartar and baking soda. Add the lukewarm water, lukewarm milk, oil and soaked millet and stir together until combined. Let sit for 8 minutes, until thickened.
3. Using cooking spray, spray a parchment-lined baking sheet and 12 English muffin rings. Place the rings on the baking sheet and scatter the farina over the pan to generously coat the surface.
4. Divide the dough into 12 equal pieces (about 4 ounces each) and place in the rings. Using greased hands, flatten gently to fit the width of the ring. Spray with cooking spray, then cover loosely with greased plastic wrap. Let rise for 1 hour.
5. Preheat the oven to 350°F with a rack in the middle. Heat a dry cast-iron skillet over medium-low heat for 3 minutes.
6. Working in batches, place 6 of the filled rings in the hot pan and cook, turning once, 5 to 8 minutes on each side. Using a spatula, transfer to the baking sheet and bake until the centers are cooked, about 6 minutes. Repeat with the remaining dough. Serve immediately. (*The cooled muffins can be stored in a resealable plastic bag for up to 3 days.*)

HAND-ROLLED BAGELS

This recipe proves that you don't have to live in a big city to get bagels fresh from the oven. I like to change up the flavors by adding different ingredients, such as cinnamon and raisins, a gluten-free whole-grain mix or crushed caraway seeds.

Makes: **6 bagels**   Prep Time: **16 minutes (plus rising)**   Cook Time: **29 minutes**

1 recipe My Gluten-Free Bagel and Pretzel Mix (page 198)

2½ teaspoons salt

2 cups lukewarm water

1 teaspoon plus 1 tablespoon brown rice syrup

1 tablespoon baking soda

1 large egg white lightly beaten with 1 tablespoon water, for egg wash

Toppings, such as poppy seeds, kosher salt, sesame seeds, caraway seeds (optional)

1. Whisk together the bagel mix and 1½ teaspoons of the salt in a large bowl. Add the lukewarm water and 1 teaspoon of the brown rice syrup; stir together until combined. Let sit for 8 minutes.

2. To shape the bagels, line a baking sheet with parchment paper and spray with cooking spray. Divide the dough into 6 equal pieces (about 4.5 ounces each). Cupping your hands, shape each into a ball. Poke a hole through the center of each and, using your thumb, rotate the dough, gradually stretching it, to form a 2-inch hole. Place the shaped dough on the baking sheet and spray with cooking spray. Cover with plastic wrap and let rest until puffy, about 1 hour.

3. About 20 minutes before baking, preheat the oven to 475°F with a rack in the middle.

4. In a large pot, bring 8 cups water to a boil. Reduce the heat to medium and stir in the baking soda, remaining 1 tablespoon brown rice syrup and remaining 1 teaspoon salt.

5. Working with a few bagels at a time, lower them into the simmering water and cook, turning once, until they have risen to the surface, about 2 minutes total. Remove with a slotted spoon and drain on a paper towel. Place, rounded side up, on the baking sheet. Brush the bagels with the egg wash and sprinkle immediately with toppings, if using.

6. Put the bagels in the oven and immediately turn the oven temperature down to 425°F. Bake the bagels until browned, about 25 minutes. Let cool on a wire rack. Serve warm or at room temperature. (*The cooled bagels can be stored in a resealable plastic bag for up to 3 days.*)

CINNAMON SUGAR CRUNCH BAGELS

These bagels were inspired by Panera Bread's famous cinnamon crunch bagels. It took me several tries before I figured out how to replicate both the crunchy cinnamon sugar coating and the tiny cinnamon morsels you get when you bite into the bagel.

Makes: **6 bagels**   Prep Time: **20 minutes (plus rising)**   Cook Time: **29 minutes**

FOR THE CINNAMON CRUNCH

- ½ cup finely crushed gluten-free rice cereal, such as Erewhon
- ¼ cup packed light brown sugar
- 1 tablespoon shortening
- 1½ teaspoons ground cinnamon
- 1½ tablespoons brown rice syrup
- ¼ teaspoon salt

FOR THE CINNAMON TOPPING

- ¼ cup granulated sugar
- ¼ cup packed light brown sugar
- 1 tablespoon ground cinnamon

FOR THE BAGELS

- 1 recipe My Gluten-Free Bagel and Pretzel Mix (page 198)
- 2½ teaspoons salt
- 2 cups lukewarm water
- 1 teaspoon plus 1 tablespoon brown rice syrup
- 1 tablespoon baking soda
- 1 large egg white lightly beaten with 1 tablespoon water, for egg wash

1. **Make the cinnamon crunch**: In a small bowl and using a fork, combine all the ingredients.
2. **Make the cinnamon topping**: In a small bowl, stir together the sugars and cinnamon.
3. **Make the bagels**: Whisk together the bagel mix and 1½ teaspoons of the salt in a large bowl. Add the lukewarm water, 1 teaspoon of the brown rice syrup and the cinnamon crunch; stir together until combined. Let sit for 8 minutes.
4. To shape the bagels, line a baking sheet with parchment paper and spray with cooking spray. Divide the dough into 6 equal pieces (about 4.5 ounces each). Cupping your hands, shape each into a ball. Poke a hole through the center of each and, using your thumb, rotate the dough, gradually stretching it, to form a 2-inch hole. Place the shaped dough on the baking sheet and spray with cooking spray. Cover with plastic wrap and let rest until puffy, about 1 hour.
5. About 20 minutes before baking, preheat the oven to $475°F°$ with a rack in the middle.
6. In a large pot, bring 8 cups water to a boil. Reduce the heat to medium and stir in the baking soda, remaining 1 tablespoon brown rice syrup and remaining 1 teaspoon salt.

7. Working with a few bagels at a time, lower them into the simmering water and cook, turning once, until they have risen to the surface, about 2 minutes total. Remove with a slotted spoon and drain on a paper towel; place, rounded side up, on the baking sheet. Brush the bagels with the egg wash and sprinkle generously with the cinnamon topping.

8. Put the bagels in the oven and immediately turn the oven temperature down to 425°F. Bake the bagels until browned, about 25 minutes. Let cool on a wire rack. Serve warm or at room temperature. *(The cooled bagels can be stored in a resealable plastic bag for up to 3 days.)*

BREADY CORN TORTILLAS

Gluten-free all-purpose flour and masa harina give these tortillas a nice chewy texture.

Makes: **12 tortillas**   Prep Time: **12 minutes**   Cook Time: **8 minutes**

- 2 cups My Gluten-Free All-Purpose Flour (page 195)
- ¾ cup masa harina
- 2 teaspoons baking powder
- ¾ teaspoon salt
- 5 tablespoons shortening
- ¾ cup plus 2 teaspoons lukewarm water

1. In a large bowl, whisk together the flour, masa harina, baking powder and salt. Add the shortening and, using your fingers or a fork, blend together until coarse crumbs form. Add the lukewarm water and stir with a fork to combine. Working on a piece of parchment paper, knead the dough until smooth. Divide into 12 pieces, shape loosely into balls and cover with plastic wrap.

2. Heat an ungreased cast-iron skillet over medium heat. On a piece of parchment, cover 1 dough ball with a piece of plastic wrap and flatten with a glass pie plate, pressing down gently and evenly in a circular motion to form a circle. Place the tortilla in the hot skillet and cook, turning once, until slightly charred, about 45 seconds on each side. Repeat with the remaining dough. To keep the tortillas warm and soft, stack them and cover with a clean dish towel. For tacos, fold them while they're still warm. *(The cooled tortillas can be stored in a resealable plastic bag between sheets of parchment for up to 3 days.)*

MULTIGRAIN LAVASH

This recipe is my healthy take on a sandwich wrap. It's packed with nutrition from the oat bran, millet, sesame seeds and almond flour, and it's conveniently bendable hot out of the oven.

Makes: **4 flatbreads**   Prep Time: **14 minutes**   Cook Time: **8 minutes**

1½ cups My Gluten-Free Sandwich Loaf Bread and Pizza Mix (page 197)

2 tablespoons gluten-free oat bran

2 tablespoons whole millet

2 tablespoons sesame seeds

2 tablespoons blanched almond flour, preferably Honeyville

1 teaspoon salt

2 teaspoons canola oil

½ cup plus 4 teaspoons water

1. Preheat the oven to 375°F with racks in the middle and upper third. Line two baking sheets with parchment paper.

2. In a large bowl, whisk together the bread mix, oat bran, millet, sesame seeds, almond flour and salt. Stir in the oil and water until combined.

3. Divide the dough into 4 pieces. Working with 1 piece on a piece of parchment paper, cover the dough with plastic wrap, flatten with your hand and, using a rolling pin, roll out to form a round about ⅛ inch thick. Place on a baking sheet and cover loosely with plastic wrap or a damp dish towel. Repeat with the remaining dough.

4. Bake the lavash until dry, but not browned, about 8 minutes. To keep warm and soft, stack the just-baked lavash and cover with a clean dish towel. If you want to stuff them, taco-style, fold them while they're still warm. (*The cooled lavash can be stored in a resealable plastic bag between sheets of parchment for up to 3 days.*)

PEPPERONI PIZZA CUPS

No need to call the pizza parlor. Part biscuit and part roll, these pizza cups will be ready in less time than it takes for the delivery guy to appear at your door. My pancake mix makes them flaky.

Makes: 12 pizza cups   **Prep Time: 8 minutes**   **Cook Time: 30 minutes**

2 cups My Gluten-Free Pancake, Waffle and Biscuit Mix (page 196)

2 teaspoons baking powder

¼ teaspoon salt

1½ cups chopped gluten-free pepperoni (about 4 ounces)

½ cup shredded dairy-free mozzarella-style cheese, plus more for topping

2 large eggs, lightly beaten

1½ cups Homemade Cashew or Almond Milk (page 205 or 206) or store-bought

¼ cup store-bought or homeade pizza sauce

1. Preheat the oven to 400°F with a rack in the middle. Generously spray a 12-cup muffin pan with cooking spray.

2. In a large bowl, whisk together the pancake mix, baking powder and salt. Add the pepperoni, mozzarella, eggs and milk; stir to combine. Gently swirl in the pizza sauce. Divide the batter among the muffin cups. Sprinkle with additional mozzarella.

3. Bake until golden and a toothpick inserted in the center comes out clean, 25 to 30 minutes. Serve immediately or at room temperature.

SALTED SOFT PRETZEL POPPERS

I used to buy the soft pretzels in the supermarket's freezer section—the bite-size variety. They were a perfect snack and easy to dip into nacho cheese sauce (page 222) or just plain yellow mustard. Now I make them myself. And they have the best qualities of both the SuperPretzel and the mall-favorite Auntie Anne's: wonderfully chewy and puffy and salty and sweet all at the same time.

Makes: About 4 dozen pretzel poppers
Cook Time: 15 minutes

Prep Time: 30 minutes (plus rising)

1 recipe My Gluten-Free Bagel and Pretzel Mix (page 198)

2 tablespoons packed light brown sugar

1 teaspoon salt, plus more for sprinkling

2 cups lukewarm water

2 tablespoons canola oil

½ cup baking soda

1 large egg beaten with 1 tablespoon water, for egg wash

Yellow mustard, for serving

1. Whisk together the pretzel mix, sugar and salt in a large bowl. Add the lukewarm water and oil; stir together to combine. Let sit for 6 minutes.

2. Cut the dough into golf ball–size pieces. Roll them into ½-inch-thick ropes and cut into 2-inch pieces. Let stand, uncovered, until puffed, about 30 minutes.

3. Meanwhile, preheat the oven to 475°F with racks in the middle and upper third. Spray two baking sheets with cooking spray. In a large pot, bring 8 cups of water and the baking soda to a boil.

4. Drop about 12 dough pieces into the boiling water and cook until they float, about 30 seconds. Remove with a slotted spoon and drain on a paper towel; place on the baking sheets. Repeat with the remaining dough, returning the water to a boil between batches.

5. Brush the dough pieces with the egg wash and sprinkle with salt. Bake until browned, about 10 minutes. Serve warm or at room temperature with mustard. (*The pretzels can be frozen in a resealable freezer bag for up to 1 month. Thaw, then reheat in a 350°F oven before serving.*)

SWEET PRETZEL POPPERS: Brush the pretzels hot from the oven with dairy-free buttery spread or unflavored coconut oil and dip to coat in cinnamon sugar (2 tablespoons ground cinnamon mixed with ½ cup sugar). Do not serve with the mustard.

CLASSIC PRETZELS: If you prefer to make a classic pretzel shape, form each dough rope into a U shape, cross the ends over each other twice to form the twist, then bring the ends to the bottom of the U and press the tips onto it. Bake until browned, about 12 minutes.

Appetizers and Salads

LET'S GET THIS MEAL STARTED

When I started to scrutinize the ingredients of appetizers like jalapeño poppers and classic salads, there was no escaping that they were loaded with gluten and dairy. So I set out to tackle them one by one, knowing that I had succeeded if I wanted to eat a whole platter. These recipes are perfect for your next Super Bowl party or for entertaining family and friends.

PUFFY BREADSTICKS WITH MARINARA SAUCE

These easy breadsticks deliver chewy-crisp memories of Pizza Hut. Sometimes I stir in about ¼ cup of my favorite pizza toppings to give the breadsticks another layer of flavor.

Makes: **12 breadsticks**   Prep Time: **12 minutes (plus rising)**   Cook Time: **20 minutes**

2 tablespoons Italian seasoning blend

3 teaspoons garlic powder

2 teaspoons salt

1 recipe My Gluten-Free Sandwich Loaf Bread and Pizza Mix (page 197), plus more for sprinkling

1 ⅓ cups water, at room temperature

2 large egg whites, lightly beaten

⅓ cup olive oil, plus more for brushing

Store-bought marinara sauce, warmed, for dipping

1. In a small bowl, stir together the Italian seasoning blend, 2 teaspoons of the garlic powder and 1 teaspoon of the salt. Set aside.

2. Preheat the oven to 400°F with racks in the middle and upper third.

3. Place the bread mix, remaining 1 teaspoon garlic powder and remaining 1 teaspoon salt in a large bowl. Add the water, egg whites and oil. Stir together with a wooden spoon until combined. Let sit until thickened, about 7 minutes.

4. Line two 9-by-13-inch baking sheets with parchment paper. Scoop the dough out onto a parchment paper-lined work surface sprinkled lightly with bread mix. Using your hands or a rolling pin, flatten the dough out to a 9-by-12-inch rectangle. Using a pizza cutter or knife, cut crosswise into 12 sticks, each about 1 inch wide.

5. Transfer to the baking sheets, brush with oil and sprinkle with the seasoning. Cover with plastic wrap and let rise at room temperature until puffy, about 1 hour.

6. Bake until golden brown, about 20 minutes. Serve hot with the marinara sauce.

CHEESY SPINACH-ARTICHOKE DIP WITH GARLIC BÉCHAMEL

A combination of homemade dairy-free béchamel, sour cream and Parmesan makes this dip extra cheesy-tasting. I serve it with tortilla chips, smear it over toasted bread or use it as a pizza topping.

Serves: **4 to 6**　　Prep Time: **12 minutes**　　Cook Time: **20 minutes**

- 1 10-ounce box frozen leaf spinach, thawed
- 1 9-ounce box frozen artichoke hearts, thawed and drained
- ¾ cup Dairy-Free Garlic Béchamel (page 210)
- ½ cup Dairy-Free Sour Cream (page 211)
- ½ teaspoon gluten-free Worcestershire sauce
- ¾ teaspoon salt
- ⅛ teaspoon black pepper
- ¼ cup finely crushed gluten-free rice cereal, such as Erewhon
- 2 tablespoons Dairy-Free Grated Parmesan (page 217) or store-bought

  Tortilla chips, for serving

1. Preheat the oven to 400°F.
2. In a small saucepan, bring 2 cups salted water to a boil. Add the spinach and artichokes and cook until tender, about 3 minutes; drain.
3. In a medium saucepan over medium heat, stir together the béchamel, sour cream, Worcestershire sauce, salt and pepper until warmed through, about 3 minutes. Stir in the spinach and artichokes to coat. Scrape the mixture into a small baking dish and sprinkle with the cereal crumbs and Parmesan. Bake until golden, about 20 minutes. Serve with tortilla chips.

JALAPEÑO POPPERS

I ate my first-ever popper at a college diner in New Paltz, New York. At the first cheese-oozing bite, I was hooked. Don't let the fact that these are dairy-free fool you. You won't be able to eat just one. I precook the jalapeños in a vinegary brine to soften them before stuffing them with a subtly seasoned mixture of dairy-free cream cheese and cheddar-style cheese.

Makes: 12 poppers   Prep Time: 14 minutes   Cook Time: 15 minutes

12 jalapeño peppers

2 cups distilled white vinegar

1 cup water

2 tablespoons salt

2 teaspoons sugar

1 7-ounce wedge dairy-free cheddar-style cheese, chopped

4 ounces dairy-free cream cheese

1 teaspoon garlic powder

½ teaspoon onion powder

½ teaspoon smoked or sweet paprika

½ teaspoon cornstarch

Canola oil, for frying

¾ cup finely crushed gluten-free rice cereal, such as Erewhon

4 large eggs

1. Cut a lengthwise slit from the stem to the bottom of each jalapeño. Make a crosswise incision at the stem end and split open enough to seed and devein.

2. In a medium saucepan over medium-high heat, bring the vinegar, water, salt and sugar to a boil and cook until the salt and sugar are dissolved. Remove from the heat, add the jalapeños and let sit until softened, about 10 minutes. Drain and pat dry.

3. In a food processor, pulse the chopped cheese, cream cheese, garlic powder, onion powder, paprika and cornstarch until combined. Fill each jalapeño with about 2 tablespoons of the cheese mixture, pressing the seam together to seal. Refrigerate for 10 minutes.

4. Fill a large pot with about 1 inch oil and heat over medium heat until a deep-fry thermometer registers 325°F. Line a baking sheet with parchment paper.

5. Meanwhile, place the cereal crumbs in a shallow bowl. In another shallow bowl, beat the eggs. Dip a stuffed jalapeño into the eggs, then coat with the cereal crumbs. Dip in the eggs and crumbs again for a double coat and place on the prepared baking sheet. Repeat with the remaining jalapeños. In batches fry the peppers, turning occasionally, until they are golden brown and the cheese is melted, 3 to 5 minutes. Remove with a slotted spoon and drain on paper towels. Return the oil to 325°F between batches.

VARIATION

BAKED JALAPEÑO POPPERS: Preheat the oven to 425°F and lightly grease a baking sheet with olive oil. Bake the stuffed and coated jalapeños, turning halfway through, until crunchy and golden, about 20 minutes.

FRIED CHEESY BALLS WITH MARINARA SAUCE

I longed for dairy-free fried mozzarella sticks, like the ones from the freezer section of the super-market or at a chain restaurant. I wanted a gooey, melty consistency when I took the first bite and that's exactly what I got.

Makes: **12 balls**   Prep Time: **8 minutes**   Cook Time: **5 minutes**

My Gluten-Free All-Purpose Flour (page 195), for coating

½ cup finely crushed gluten-free rice cereal, such as Erewhon

1½ teaspoons dried parsley flakes

2 large eggs, beaten

2 tablespoons Homemade Cashew or Almond Milk (page 205 or 206) or store-bought

1 7-ounce wedge dairy-free cheddar-style or Jack-style cheese, cubed and rolled into balls

Canola oil, for frying

Store-bought marinara sauce, warmed, for serving

1. Place about ½ cup flour in a shallow bowl. Stir together the cereal crumbs and parsley in another shallow bowl. Beat together the eggs and milk in a third shallow bowl.

2. Dip the cheese balls in the flour, then in the eggs, then in the cereal crumbs, turning to coat completely. Dip in the eggs and crumbs again for a double coat.

3. Heat 1½ inches oil in a deep saucepan over medium-high heat until it registers 350°F on a deep-fry thermometer.

4. Add the cheese balls to the hot oil in batches and fry, turning, until golden, about 1½ minutes. Transfer with a slotted spoon to a wire rack set over a baking pan. Serve with the marinara sauce.

LOADED NACHO POTATO SKINS WITH HOMEMADE REFRIED BEANS

Keep naked potato skins on hand so you can enjoy these whenever you want to. When you make potato skins at home instead of ordering them in a restaurant, there's no chance of cross contamination from gluten. Usually, I prefer fresh herbs over dried, but there's something about the dried oregano and thyme that gives these potato skins their authentic flavor.

Makes: 8 potato skins   **Prep Time: 15 minutes**   **Cook Time: 1 hour 35 minutes**

4 russet potatoes

2 tablespoons olive oil, plus more for rubbing

Salt

2 tablespoons finely chopped onion

1 garlic clove, finely chopped

1 jalapeño pepper, halved and seeded (optional)

¼ teaspoon dried oregano

¼ teaspoon dried thyme

1 15-ounce can pinto beans, rinsed and drained

½ cup water

Hot sauce (optional)

Store-bought salsa

Sliced black olives

Dairy-Free Sour Cream (page 211) or store-bought

Chopped fresh cilantro or scallions

1. Preheat the oven to 400°F.

2. Using a fork, poke the potatoes in a few places, then rub with oil and sprinkle with salt. Bake until crispy outside and creamy inside, about 1 hour. (Leave the oven on.) Let cool slightly, then halve length- wise and scoop out some of the potato (save for another use), leaving about a ¼-inch-thick skin. Rub the inside of the potato shell with oil and bake until crispy and golden, about 20 minutes. (*The potato shells can be refrigerated, covered, for up to 2 days.*)

3. Meanwhile, in a medium skillet, heat the 2 tablespoons oil over medium heat. Add the onion, garlic, jalapeño (if using), oregano, thyme and ¼ teaspoon salt. Cook, stirring occasionally, until the onions are golden and softened. Add the beans and water. Remove the jalapeño, if using, and mash the beans with the back of a wooden spoon. Cook, stirring occasionally and adding more water if necessary, until the beans reach the desired consistency, about 15 minutes; season with salt and hot sauce, if using. (*The beans will keep, covered, in the fridge for 1 week. Reheat before serving.*)

4. To serve, top the potato skins with the beans, salsa, olives, sour cream and cilantro.

Crispy Shrimp and Pork Potstickers wtih Chili Soy Dipping Sauce (page 76)

CRISPY SHRIMP AND PORK POTSTICKERS WITH CHILI-SOY DIPPING SAUCE

I tried store-bought frozen gluten-free dumplings, but they weren't great and stuck to the pan. I was intimidated at the prospect of making them myself since I had never made dumpling dough before. The first few tries yielded a dough that wouldn't hold together. The solution turned out to be sweet rice flour. These potstickers will not stick to your pan, and they're delicious.

Makes: **About 36 potstickers**   Prep Time: **45 minutes**   Cook Time: **35 minutes**

FOR THE SHRIMP FILLING

- 6 Napa cabbage leaves, finely shredded
- 1 teaspoon salt
- ½ pound shrimp, peeled, deveined and coarsely chopped
- ½ pound ground pork
- 2 tablespoons cornstarch
- ½ teaspoon black pepper
- 2 scallions, finely chopped
- 2 garlic cloves, finely chopped
- 1 tablespoon finely chopped peeled fresh ginger
- 1 tablespoon chopped fresh cilantro
- 2 tablespoons gluten-free tamari
- 1 tablespoon toasted sesame oil

FOR THE DUMPLINGS

- 1¼ cups My Gluten-Free All-Purpose Flour (page 195), plus more for dusting
- ¾ cup gluten-free sweet rice flour
- ¾ teaspoon salt
- ¾ cup plus 2 tablespoons boiling water

FOR THE DIPPING SAUCE

- ¼ cup sweet gluten-free chili sauce
- ¼ cup gluten-free tamari
- 2 teaspoons rice vinegar
- 1 teaspoon sesame seeds
- 1 teaspoon grated peeled fresh ginger
- 1 jalapeño pepper, seeded and sliced into thin rounds
- 2 tablespoons canola oil

1. **Make the shrimp filling**: In a small bowl, toss together the cabbage and salt. Let wilt for about 10 minutes, then drain and squeeze dry. In a medium bowl, combine the cabbage and the remaining ingredients. Refrigerate, covered, until ready to use.

2. **Make the dumplings**: Meanwhile, in a food processor, process the flours and salt. With the motor running, slowly stream in the boiling water until a dough forms. Divide into 2 pieces and place in a resealable plastic bag. Working with 1 piece of dough at a time on a flour-dusted piece of parchment paper and, using your hands, roll the dough into a

rope about $^3/_4$ inch in diameter. Cut into rounds about $^3/_4$ inch thick and return to the resealable bag.

3. Working with 1 round of dough at a time and with the palm of your hand, press down gently to flatten. Using a lightly floured rolling pin, roll out to form a circle about $^1/_{16}$ inch thick. Place about 1 tablespoon filling in the center and, using your finger, wet half of the edge with water. Fold the dough over to form a half-moon and pinch or pleat to seal completely. Place on a parchment-lined baking sheet.

4. **Make the dipping sauce**: In a small bowl, stir together all the ingredients.

5. Meanwhile, in a large nonstick frying pan with a tight-fitting lid, heat the oil over medium-high heat until hot but not smoking. Add about half of the dumplings to the pan and fry until crunchy and golden, about 3 minutes. Carefully pour in $^1/_3$ cup water to the pan and cover immediately. Reduce the heat to medium-low and steam until cooked through, about 12 minutes. Uncover, turn up the heat to medium-high and cook until the water evaporates. Repeat with the remaining dumplings. Serve with the dipping sauce.

SALT-AND-PEPPER FRIED CALAMARI

I don't add salt to the flour coating since it would draw the moisture out of the squid, turning an otherwise crunchy coating soggy. Instead, I sprinkle a peppery coarse-salt mixture over the fried squid as it comes out of the oil. Monitor the temperature of the oil with a deep-fry thermometer and fry in small batches so the temperature doesn't drop suddenly, or the squid will absorb excess oil. If the temperature starts to fall, return the oil to 375°F before frying the next batch. If the temperature gets too hot, carefully remove the pot from the heat before continuing. To keep the fried squid warm, place on a baking sheet, uncovered, in a 200°F oven.

Serves: 4   Prep Time: 15 minutes   Cook Time: 18 minutes

Vegetable oil, for frying

1 teaspoon coarse salt

1 teaspoon black pepper

1 teaspoon crushed red pepper flakes

½ teaspoon sugar (optional)

½ cup My Gluten-Free All-Purpose Flour (page 195)

1 cup cornstarch

1 pound cleaned fresh squid, cut into ⅓-inch-wide rings (do not pat dry)

Sweet (or hot) gluten-free Thai chili sauce, for serving

Lime wedges, for serving

1. Fill a deep, heavy-bottomed skillet with 1 inch oil and heat over medium heat until it registers 375°F on a deep-fry thermometer.

2. In a small bowl, stir together the salt, black pepper, red pepper flakes and sugar, if using. Set aside.

3. Meanwhile, combine the flour and cornstarch in a large bowl. Add the squid and toss. Working in batches, transfer the squid to a sieve or colander and shake to remove any excess flour.

4. Submerge about 6 of the coated squid pieces into the heated oil and fry, turning, until crisp and golden, about 3 minutes. Using a slotted spoon or tongs, transfer to paper towels to drain. Sprinkle with the pepper mixture. Let the oil return to 375°F before frying the next batch. Repeat with the remaining squid. Serve with chili sauce and lime wedges.

MUSSELS MARINARA

When I make mussels at home, I keep things simple with a basic marinara sauce. The wine is a tad fancy, but it makes for a rich sauce that you want to slurp up with the shells. The mussels and sauce are also great tossed with pasta.

Serves: **4**   Prep Time: **10 minutes**   Cook Time: **10 minutes**

2   tablespoons olive oil

2   garlic cloves, smashed

1   28-ounce can tomato puree (about 2 cups)

½   cup dry red wine

2   tablespoons chili powder

    Salt

2   pounds mussels, rinsed and debearded

¼   cup chopped fresh parsley

1. In a large saucepan, heat the oil over medium-high heat. Add the garlic and cook, stirring, until golden, about 1 minute. Add the tomato puree, wine and chili powder. Cook, stirring occasionally, until the alcohol evaporates, about 3 minutes. Season with salt.

2. Stir in the mussels, cover and cook until they open, about 3 minutes. Remove the mussels to a bowl. Cook any mussels that do not open a little longer and, if they still do not open, discard. Return the mussels to the pan, sprinkle with the parsley and serve.

CRISPY CHICKEN TAQUITOS

The chipotles in adobo sauce and fire-roasted tomatoes give the chicken heat and smokiness. If you can get your hands on Mexican oregano, which is more subtle and earthier than other varieties, use it. I like to make a double batch and freeze some for later.

To soften the tortillas, wrap them in a damp dish towel or paper towels and microwave for about 30 seconds, until soft and pliable. Or, place the tortillas on a baking sheet in stacks of two and generously brush both sides with oil. Bake in a 350°F oven, turning them once, to soften and warm, about 3 minutes.

Makes: **12 taquitos**   Prep Time: **11 minutes**   Cook Time: **16 minutes**

1 15-ounce can diced fire-roasted tomatoes, drained

½ medium onion, chopped

1 garlic clove, peeled

2 chipotle peppers in adobo sauce or 1 jalapeño pepper, seeded and chopped

½ teaspoon dried oregano

¾ teaspoon salt

3 cups shredded cooked chicken

3 tablespoons finely chopped fresh cilantro or parsley

Canola oil, for frying

12 6-inch corn tortillas, warmed to soften (see headnote)

Dairy-Free Sour Cream (page 211), homeade or store-bought salsa and guacamole, for serving

1. In a blender, puree the tomatoes, onion, garlic, chipotles and oregano until smooth. Transfer to a medium skillet and bring to a boil. Reduce the heat and simmer, stirring occasionally, for about 5 minutes. Season with the salt. Stir in the chicken and cilantro.

2. In a large pan over medium-high heat, heat ½ inch oil until it registers 350°F on a deep-fry thermometer. Meanwhile, spoon about 2 tablespoons chicken filling onto 1 warm tortilla, leaving a ½-inch border. Roll up and secure with a toothpick. Repeat with the remaining tortillas. *(You will only use half the filling; freeze the rest for later.)*

3. Working with 3 taquitos at a time, add to the hot oil and fry, turning once, until golden, about 4 minutes. Drain on paper towels, remove the toothpicks and serve with the sour cream, salsa and guacamole. *(The taquitos can be made ahead and frozen in a single layer in a resealable freezer bag. To reheat, place on a greased baking sheet in a single layer and bake in a 400°F oven, turning once, until crunchy, about 20 minutes.)*

BAKED CHICKEN TAQUITOS: Preheat the oven to 350°F. Line a baking sheet with parchment paper and spray it lightly with cooking spray. Place the rolled-up taquitos seam side down on the baking sheet in a single layer. Spray the tops lightly with cooking spray or brush with oil. Sprinkle with a pinch of salt. Bake until crisp and the ends start to turn golden brown, 15 to 20 minutes.

BAKED HONEY BARBECUE POPCORN CHICKEN

Every time my father traveled for business, my mom—who would normally make a home-cooked dinner for us every single night—would pull out all of the freezer stops. Popcorn chicken served alongside mac and cheese was one of our favorites. To give my version a ton of flavor, I use both my seasoned flour and bread crumb mix.

Serves: **4**   Prep Time: **10 minutes**   Cook Time: **8 minutes**

1 pound chicken tenders or boneless, skinless chicken breasts (about 3 breasts)

Salt and black pepper

½ cup My Gluten-Free Seasoned Flour (page 199)

4 large egg whites

¼ cup Homemade Cashew or Almond Milk (page 205 or 206)

2 cups My Gluten-Free Bread Crumbs (page 200) or finely crushed gluten-free rice cereal, such as Erewhon

½ cup ketchup

¼ cup honey

1 tablespoon gluten-free Worcestershire sauce

1. Preheat the oven to 475°F and place a wire rack on a baking sheet. Spray with cooking spray.
2. Cut the chicken into bite-size pieces and season with salt and pepper. Place the seasoned flour in a large resealable bag. Add the chicken pieces and shake to coat.
3. In a small bowl, whisk together the egg whites and milk until combined.
4. Place the bread crumbs in a shallow plate. Dip the coated chicken into the egg-white mixture, then toss to coat with the bread crumbs. Repeat to make a double coat. Place on the rack and spray the chicken with cooking spray.
5. Bake, turning the pieces once, until cooked through and crisp, about 8 minutes.
6. In a small bowl, stir together the ketchup, honey and Worcestershire sauce. Season with salt and pepper. Toss the popcorn chicken in the honey barbecue sauce and serve. *(The popcorn chicken can be made ahead and frozen in a single layer in a resealable freezer bag. To reheat, place on a greased baking sheet in a single layer and bake in a 375°F oven, turning once, until crunchy, about 15 minutes total.)*

FRIED HONEY BARBECUE POPCORN CHICKEN:
Heat 2 inches oil in a deep skillet over medium
heat to 350°F. In batches, carefully add the
coated chicken and fry, turning once, until
golden brown and cooked through, about
2 minutes on each side. Drain on paper towels
and season with salt.

CORN DOG NUGGETS

You can find gluten-free hot dogs at the supermarket, but gluten-free corn dogs? Not yet. I prefer medium-grind cornmeal for the textural crunch and extra corniness it gives the nuggets. I generally boil the hot dogs, but a char flavor from the grill adds a wonderfully smoky layer of flavor.

Makes: **24 nuggets**   Prep Time: **10 minutes**   Cook Time: **8 minutes**

2 tablespoons canola oil, plus more for frying

1 cup My Gluten-Free All-Purpose Flour (page 195)

8 gluten-free beef hot dogs, boiled or grilled, cooled and cut into thirds

1½ cups cornmeal, preferably medium-grind

2 teaspoons baking powder

1 teaspoon sugar

1½ teaspoons salt

½ teaspoon chili powder

½ teaspoon onion powder

2 large eggs

1 cup milk

Mustard, ketchup, relish and hot sauce, for serving

1. Heat about 3 inches oil to 350°F in a deep pot over medium-high heat.

2. Scatter ¼ cup of the flour on a plate. Roll the hot dog pieces in the flour to coat; shake off any excess.

3. In a medium bowl, whisk together the remaining ¾ cup flour, cornmeal, baking powder, sugar, salt, chili powder and onion powder. Whisk in the 2 tablespoons oil, the eggs and milk.

4. Working in batches of 6, submerge each floured hot dog in the batter to coat completely, then add to the hot oil and fry, turning occasionally, until golden and crispy, about 2 minutes. Transfer to paper towels to drain. Between batches, return the oil to 350°F. Serve hot with the condiments of choice. (*The corn dog nuggets can be made ahead and frozen in a single layer in a resealable freezer bag. To reheat, place on a greased baking sheet in a single layer and bake in a 375°F oven, turning once, until crunchy, about 20 minutes.*)

EGGPLANT TERIYAKI

I prefer to make my own teriyaki sauce so I can control not just the gluten, but the flavor. Orange zest and juice, brown sugar and ginger contribute just the right amount of sweetness and provide a nice tang. If you're pressed for time, use store-bought gluten-free teriyaki sauce. Serve steamed rice alongside if you'd like to serve this as a main dish.

Serves: **4**   Prep Time: **5 minutes (plus marinating)**   Cook Time: **25 minutes**

4 medium eggplants, stemmed, ends trimmed, halved lengthwise

1 cup Orange-Ginger Teriyaki Sauce (recipe follows) or store-bought gluten-free teriyaki sauce

4 tablespoons olive oil

Sesame seeds, for serving

1. Score the cut side of the eggplants in a criss-cross pattern, making sure not to cut all the way through.

2. Generously brush the eggplants on the cut side with some of the teriyaki sauce. Marinate for about 30 minutes. *(The eggplant can be covered and refrigerated overnight).*

3. In a large nonstick skillet, heat 2 tablespoons of the oil over medium heat. Place half of the eggplants in the skillet, cut sides up, and brush on more teriyaki sauce. Cook, uncovered and turning once, until softened and caramelized, 10 to 12 minutes. Repeat with the remaining 2 tablespoons oil, eggplants and teriyaki sauce. Sprinkle with the sesame seeds and serve.

ORANGE-GINGER TERIYAKI SAUCE

Use this sweet and tangy sauce with beef or chicken in addition to the eggplant. If you don't have mirin, a Japanese sweet rice wine, substitute 1 tablespoon sugar plus ¼ cup white wine or dry sherry.

Makes: About 1½ cups • **Prep Time: 5 minutes** • **Cook Time: 15 minutes**

½ cup gluten-free tamari

¼ cup mirin

¼ cup homemade or store-bought vegetable broth, chicken broth or water

¼ cup packed light brown sugar

1 tablespoon vegetable oil

1 tablespoon rice wine vinegar or apple cider vinegar

4 garlic cloves, chopped

1 tablespoon grated peeled fresh ginger (about 1-inch piece)

Zest and juice of 1 orange

2 teaspoons cornstarch dissolved in 2 tablespoons water

Combine all the ingredients except the cornstarch mixture in a blender and process until smooth. Transfer to a saucepan and bring to a boil. Reduce the heat to medium–low and simmer until slightly thickened, about 10 minutes. Stir in the cornstarch mixture and return to a boil. Cook, stirring, until glossy, about 5 minutes. Let cool. *(The teriyaki sauce can be made ahead of time and refrigerated for up to 1 month.)*

TEX-MEX WEDGES WITH
CREAMY JALAPEÑO DRESSING

Jalapeño pepper gives this salad a kick. A hint of cumin in the dressing contributes a nice smokiness, especially when combined with quintessential Tex-Mex ingredients like corn, beans and cilantro. Want more crunch? Sprinkle 2 slices of cooked, crumbled bacon on top.

Serves: **4**   Prep Time: **8 minutes**

FOR THE DRESSING

- 2 jalapeño peppers, stemmed, seeded and chopped
- ¼ cup Dairy-Free Mayonnaise (page 221) or Dairy-Free Sour Cream (page 211) or store-bought
- 1 garlic clove, smashed
- 2 tablespoons fresh cilantro or parsley
- Juice of 1 lime (about 2 tablespoons)
- 1 tablespoon honey
- ¼ teaspoon ground cumin
- ¼ cup olive oil
- Salt

FOR THE SALAD

- 1 head iceberg lettuce, quartered
- 1 15-ounce can black beans, rinsed and drained
- 2 medium tomatoes, peeled and cut into wedges
- 1 ripe avocado, pitted, peeled and cut into wedges
- 1 red bell pepper, ribs and seeds removed, chopped
- 1 cup raw or cooked corn kernels (from 2 ears, or frozen and thawed)
- 4 radishes, thinly sliced

1. **Make the dressing**: In a blender, blend the jalapeños, mayonnaise, garlic, cilantro, lime juice, honey and cumin. With the motor running, stream in the oil and blend until creamy, about 30 seconds. Season with about ½ teaspoon salt. *(The dressing will keep, covered, in the fridge for up to 3 days.)*

2. **Make the salad**: Place a lettuce wedge on its side on each of four plates. Top with the beans, tomatoes, avocado, bell pepper and corn. Drizzle with the dressing and scatter the radish slices over the top. Serve.

ICEBOX QUINOA "MACARONI" SALAD

My friend Emiko Shimojo brought this salad to my house one day. I loved it so much that I not only asked her for the recipe, but also asked her if I could share it. Who knew that quinoa would be such a wonderful substitute for classic macaroni pasta? I also love the mayonnaise-based dressing, which gets just enough acidity from Dijon mustard and red wine vinegar.

Serves: **4** • Prep Time: **12 minutes** • Cook Time: **15 minutes**

2½ cups water

Salt

2 cups quinoa

½ cup Dairy-Free Mayonnaise (page 221) or store-bought

1 tablespoon Dijon mustard

1 tablespoon red wine vinegar

½ English cucumber, cut into quarters and thinly sliced

1 cup grape tomatoes, halved

4 carrots, peeled and thinly sliced into rounds

4 scallions, thinly sliced

Black pepper

1. In a small saucepan, bring the water and 2 teaspoons salt to a boil. Stir in the quinoa, cover and cook over low heat until the water is absorbed, about 15 minutes. Remove from the heat and let sit, covered, for 5 minutes.

2. In a large bowl, whisk together the mayonnaise, mustard and vinegar. Add the cooked quinoa, cucumber, tomatoes, carrots and scallions and toss to coat evenly. Season with salt and pepper. Refrigerate until chilled, at least 1 hour.

SEVEN-LAYER SHRIMP TOSTADA SALAD WITH SOUR CREAM–LIME DRESSING

This naturally gluten-free salad is easy to assemble. It features a few of the traditional seven layers—iceberg lettuce, tomatoes and bacon. I put my own spin on it by adding briny olives and creamy avocado.

Serves: **4**   Prep Time: **12 minutes**   Cook Time: **3 minutes**

1 pound large shrimp, peeled, deveined and tails discarded

½ cup Dairy-Free Sour Cream (page 211) or store-bought

2 tablespoons lime juice, plus 1 lime, halved, for squeezing

½ teaspoon ground cumin

¼ cup olive oil

¼ cup chopped fresh cilantro or parsley

Salt and black pepper

1 head iceberg lettuce, thinly sliced

1 15-ounce can black beans, rinsed and drained

1 cup raw or cooked corn kernels (from 2 ears or frozen and thawed)

3 cups chopped tomatoes

1 6-ounce can sliced pitted black olives, drained

2 ripe avocados, pitted, peeled and chopped

6 slices bacon, cooked until crisp and crumbled (optional)

Homemade Tortilla Chips (recipe follows) or store-bought, broken into large pieces, for topping

1. Bring a large pot of generously salted water to a boil. Add the shrimp, cover and remove the pot from the heat. Let stand until the shrimp are cooked through, about 3 minutes. Drain, pat dry and refrigerate.

2. Combine the sour cream, lime juice and cumin in a small bowl. In a slow, steady stream, whisk in the oil. Stir in the cilantro and season with salt and pepper.

3. Scatter the sliced lettuce over the bottom of a big glass bowl. Top with the beans, corn, tomatoes, olives and avocados. Squeeze some lime juice over the salad, then top with the cooked shrimp and bacon. Pour the dressing over the top and spread to cover the salad. Refrigerate for at least 1 hour or overnight. To serve, top with the broken tortilla chips.

VARIATION

SEVEN-LAYER CHICKEN OR TOFU TOSTADAS: If you like, swap out the shrimp for shredded, cooked chicken or chopped store-bought firm smoked tofu.

HOMEMADE TORTILLA CHIPS

Serves: **6** • Prep Time: **5 minutes** • Cook Time: **12 minutes**

12 6-inch corn tortillas

Olive oil or cooking spray

Salt

Finely grated zest of 1 lime
(optional)

1. Preheat the oven to 400°F with the racks in the middle and upper third.
2. Brush both sides of the tortillas with oil or spray with cooking spray. Stack the tortillas and cut into sixths. Place in a single layer on two baking sheets. Sprinkle generously with salt.
3. Bake until crisp and golden, 10 to 12 minutes. Gently toss with the lime zest, if using. Let cool completely, then store in a resealable plastic bag for up to 1 week.

CHINESE CHICKEN SALAD

I've never had a Chinese chicken salad that I liked more than this one. The flavors are wonderfully complex and the raw vegetables give it great crunch.

Serves: **4**   Prep Time: **15 minutes**

¼ cup gluten-free tamari

¼ cup well-stirred tahini

¼ cup unseasoned rice vinegar or apple cider vinegar

1 garlic clove, chopped

1 tablespoon chopped peeled fresh ginger

1½ teaspoons salt

½ teaspoon pepper

1 tablespoon sesame oil

½ cup canola oil

1 10-ounce bag shredded coleslaw mix (4 cups)

¼ pound snow peas, trimmed and sliced lengthwise

1 medium cucumber, peeled, seeded and chopped

2 carrots, peeled and coarsely grated

2 scallions, sliced

2 tablespoons chopped fresh cilantro or parsley

3 cups shredded cooked chicken

2 oranges, peeled, white pith removed, and cut between the membranes to remove segments

½ cup slivered almonds, toasted

2 tablespoons sesame seeds, toasted

1. In a blender, process the tamari, tahini, vinegar, garlic, ginger, salt and pepper until combined. Stream in the sesame oil and canola oil and blend until smooth.

2. In a large bowl, toss together the coleslaw mix, snow peas, cucumber, carrots, scallions and cilantro.

3. Add the dressing and toss to combine. Transfer to a serving platter. Top with the chicken, oranges, almonds and sesame seeds and serve.

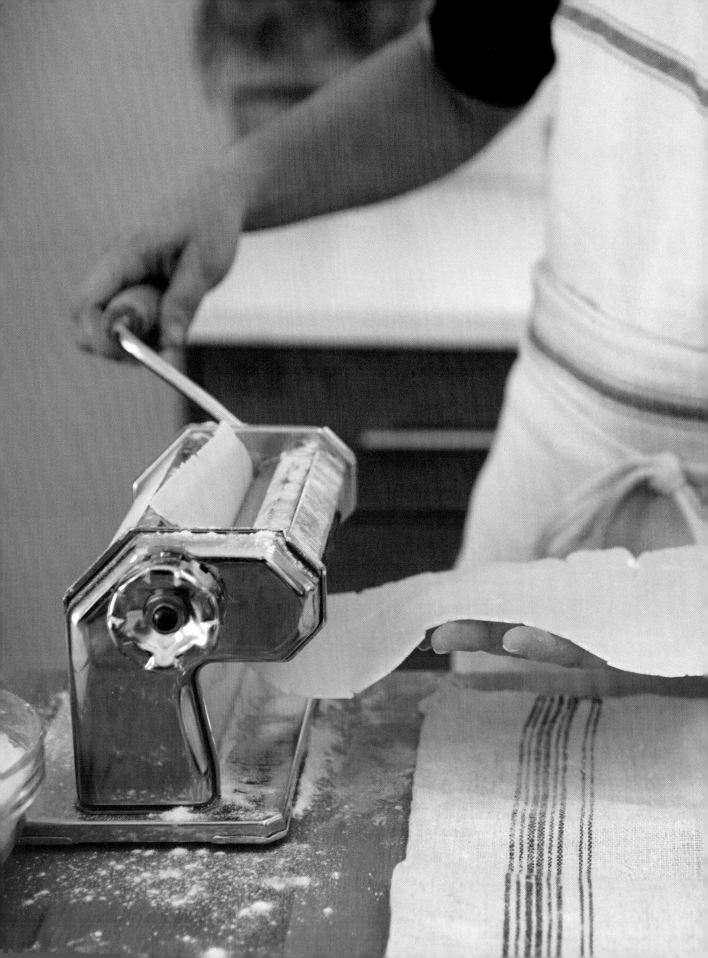

Soups, Pasta and Rice

YOU'LL BE BOWLED OVER

I wanted to salvage my son's Italian culinary heritage with a big plate of pasta. I began playing around with gluten-free flours, and we went from eating mushy noodles (or none at all) to plates steaming with homemade fresh pasta. Supermarkets have expanded their gluten-free pasta offerings greatly, and I'm happy to say that there are a couple of brands (page 6) that I keep in my pantry for a weeknight meal.

AVOCADO GAZPACHO WITH PEACHES AND CORN

I was never a fan of gazpacho. That is, until I made it myself. Now I realize that the soup can be refreshing and as bold as you want it to be. I prepare it only at the height of summer when I can find tomatoes bursting with flavor, and I stir in as much of summer as I can: watermelon, corn and peaches.

Serve with crushed tortilla chips—or dress up with poached shrimp or lobster. If the gazpacho thickens too much, gradually add water until it reaches your desired consistency, then season with salt as necessary.

Serves: **8** · Prep Time: **15 minutes (plus chilling)**

3 large tomatoes (about 2 pounds), cored and chopped

1 small onion, chopped

1 bell pepper, seeded and chopped

1 cucumber, peeled, seeded and chopped

2 cups tomato juice

1 cup watermelon or orange juice

2 tablespoons sherry vinegar or red wine vinegar

1 cup raw or cooked corn (from 2 ears or frozen and thawed)

1 peach, pitted and chopped

2 ripe avocados, pitted, peeled and chopped

   Salt and black pepper

1 jalapeño pepper, seeded and chopped, to taste

½ cup chopped fresh cilantro or parsley

2 limes, quartered, for serving

1. Working in batches, pulse the tomatoes, onion, bell pepper and cucumber in a food processor until chunky. Transfer to a large bowl and stir in the tomato juice, watermelon juice and vinegar. Stir in the corn, peach and avocado. Season with salt and pepper.

2. Refrigerate until completely chilled, at least 3 hours or overnight. Stir in the jalapeño and cilantro. Serve with the lime wedges.

CHICKEN CUP OF NOODLES

Convenience-store ramen noodle soup was one of my college staples. When I went to re-create it, I had no idea how I was going to mimic the chicken flavor. From the ingredient label, I learned that turmeric gives the classic its color. But perhaps the most surprising ingredient besides chicken powder was soy sauce. I added some gluten-free tamari and soon I had a soothing meal that is almost as quick as my dorm-room version. Make sure you read the ingredient label if you're buying chicken broth since some brands add starch—including regular flour—to add body.

Serves: **4 to 6**   Prep Time: **6 minutes**   Cook Time: **20 minutes**

1 quart homemade or store-bought chicken broth

2 cups water

2 teaspoons gluten-free tamari

1 teaspoon sugar (optional)

1 teaspoon onion powder

1 teaspoon garlic powder

½ teaspoon ground turmeric

Salt

8 ounces gluten-free brown rice ramen noodles, such as Lotus Foods

2 cups cooked cubed or shredded chicken

¼ cup chopped carrot (about 1 carrot)

¼ cup frozen peas

¼ cup frozen corn

1. In a soup pot over medium heat, combine the broth, water, tamari, sugar (if using), onion powder, garlic powder and turmeric. Season with about 1 teaspoon salt and bring to a boil.

2. Add the noodles and simmer until tender, about 3 minutes. Stir in the chicken, carrot, peas and corn and continue to cook until heated through, about 5 minutes. Serve hot.

SMOKY SPLIT PEA SOUP WITH MUSTARD CROUTONS

The smokiness of my mom's pea soup came from cubed ham. I like to add some chipotle pepper puree instead, which works well if you have vegetarians in the house. (Just make sure to use vegetable broth.) To make the soup heartier for meat eaters, stir in cooked, cubed ham steak before serving. Looking to spice things up? Add 1 seeded, chopped jalapeño to the mix.

Serves: 4 **Prep Time: 14 minutes** **Cook Time: 1 hour 20 minutes**

6 tablespoons olive oil

2 carrots, chopped

2 celery stalks, peeled and chopped

1 large onion, chopped

Salt and black pepper

2 teaspoons mustard powder

½ teaspoon turmeric

1 tablespoon chipotle pepper adobo sauce puree, or to taste

1 1-pound bag split peas, picked over and rinsed

2 quarts homemade or store-bought chicken or vegetable broth

6 slices Sandwich Loaf Bread (page 40) or store-bought, crusts removed and cut into 1-inch pieces (about 3 cups)

2 tablespoons Dijon mustard

1 teaspoon whole-grain mustard

1. In a large pot, heat 2 tablespoons of the oil over medium heat. Add the carrots, celery and onion. Season with salt and pepper and cook, stirring, until softened, about 6 minutes. Stir in the mustard powder, turmeric and chipotle pepper puree and cook for 1 minute. Stir in the split peas and broth. Reduce the heat to medium–low, partially cover and simmer, stirring occasionally, until the peas start to break down, adding more broth or water as needed, about 1 hour. *(The soup can be refrigerated for up to 3 days or frozen for up to 1 month.)*

2. Meanwhile, preheat the oven to 350°F with a rack in the middle.

3. On a baking sheet, toss together the remaining 4 tablespoons oil, bread, mustards and ¼ teaspoon salt until coated. Spread out evenly. Bake, stirring halfway through, until the croutons are golden and crisp, about 15 minutes.

4. To serve, divide the soup among four shallow bowls and top with mustard croutons.

CREAMY KALE-CANNELLINI SOUP WITH GARLIC CHIPS

The flavors in this soup remind me of the Italian countryside, and they only get better overnight—that is, if you're lucky enough to have any leftovers. The cannellini beans give a creamy texture. Garlic chips add a welcome crunch; I learned how to make them from watching my mom. If you prefer your soup a little thinner, just add water and a pinch of salt. Looking to make a one-pot meal out of this recipe? Add sliced cooked Italian sausages, cooked meatballs or cubed extra-firm tofu.

Serves: **4**   Prep Time: **12 minutes**   Cook Time: **26 minutes**

4 tablespoons olive oil

2 celery stalks, chopped

1 onion, chopped

2 garlic cloves, crushed, plus 2 garlic cloves, thinly sliced

1 tablespoon chopped mixed fresh herbs, such as thyme, rosemary and parsley

¼ teaspoon crushed red pepper flakes (optional)

2 15-ounce cans cannellini beans, rinsed and drained

4 cups homemade or store-bought chicken or vegetable broth

1 pound kale, stems and center ribs discarded and leaves finely chopped

1½ teaspoons salt

¾ teaspoon black pepper

1. In a large saucepan, heat 2 tablespoons of the oil over medium-high heat. Add the celery, onion, crushed garlic, herbs and red pepper. Cook until softened, about 5 minutes.

2. Add about half of the beans and 1 cup of the broth. Mash the beans with a fork or potato masher. Add the remaining 3 cups broth and bring to a boil. Stir in the remaining half of the beans, kale, salt and pepper. Reduce the heat to medium-low, cover partially and simmer until the kale is tender, about 20 minutes.

3. Meanwhile, heat the remaining 2 tablespoons oil in a small skillet over medium-low heat. Add the sliced garlic and cook, stirring often, until crisp and golden, about 1 minute. Drain on paper towels.

4. Divide the soup among four bowls, top each serving with garlic chips and serve.

NACHOS MAC-AND-CHEESE

This recipe combines two of my favorite dishes. You won't notice that there isn't any dairy in the warm cheesy-tasting nacho sauce.

Serves: 8   Prep Time: **10 minutes**   Cook Time: **10 minutes**

1   12-ounce box gluten-free elbow macaroni

¼   cup canola oil

1   garlic clove, chopped

1   cup finely crushed tortilla chips

½   teaspoon salt

2   tablespoons finely chopped fresh cilantro or parsley

1½   cups Dairy-Free Nacho Cheese Sauce (page 222), warmed

1. In a large saucepan of boiling salted water, cook the macaroni until al dente; drain.

2. Meanwhile, heat the oil in a medium skillet over medium heat. Stir in the garlic, tortilla chip crumbs and salt. Toast until crisp and golden, about 5 minutes. Remove from the heat and stir in the cilantro.

3. Place the nacho sauce in a large serving bowl and stir in the cooked macaroni. Serve, sprinkling some of the tortilla crumb mixture over each portion.

VARIATION

EXTRA-CHEESY NACHOS MAC-AND-CHEESE:
For extra cheesiness, transfer the cooked mac-and-cheese to a baking dish, top with shredded dairy-free cheddar and the tortilla crumbs, then finish in a 400°F oven until the cheese is melted.

PASTA CAPONATA

Caponata is a classic Sicilian eggplant dish typically served as an appetizer or side dish, but here I toss it with pasta. It gets its briny, sweet-and-sour flavor from capers, olives, balsamic vinegar and sugar. The fresh basil stirred in at the last minute brightens the dish.

Serves: **4**   Prep Time: **12 minutes**   Cook Time: **42 minutes**

- 6 tablespoons olive oil
- ¼ teaspoon crushed red pepper, or to taste
- 4 small eggplants (about 1½ pounds), partially peeled and cut into ½-inch pieces (about 3 cups)
- 2 zucchini, cut into ½-inch pieces (about 2 cups)
- 1 large red onion, cut into ½-inch pieces (about 1½ cups)
- 2 medium celery stalks, finely chopped (about 1 cup)
- Salt
- 2 tablespoons sugar, or to taste
- ½ cup pitted kalamata olives
- 2 tablespoons salt-packed capers, rinsed and drained
- 3 tablespoons balsamic vinegar
- 1 28-ounce can chopped tomatoes
- 1 12-ounce box gluten-free penne pasta
- ¼ cup chopped fresh basil

1. Bring a large pot of generously salted water to a boil.
2. Meanwhile, make the caponata: In a large, deep skillet, heat 4 tablespoons of the oil over medium-high heat. Add the red pepper, eggplants and zucchini; and cook, stirring frequently, until softened and golden, about 10 minutes. Transfer to a bowl and wipe out the skillet.
3. Heat the remaining 2 tablespoons oil in the skillet over medium-high heat. Add the onion, celery and ¼ teaspoon salt and cook, stirring, until softened, about 5 minutes. Stir in the sugar and continue cooking until the vegetables are caramelized, about 12 minutes. Return the eggplants and zucchini to the skillet. Stir in the olives, capers and vinegar and cook until the vinegar has evaporated. Add the tomatoes and simmer over low heat, covered and stirring occasionally, until thickened, about 20 minutes. Season with salt and transfer to a large bowl. *(The caponata can be made ahead of time and refrigerated for up to 3 days. Bring to room temperature before serving.)*
4. Add the pasta to the boiling salted water and cook until al dente, drain. Add the pasta to the caponata and toss. Stir in the basil and serve immediately.

SPAGHETTI CLAMS CASINO

I took the ingredients from the classic appetizer clams casino and incorporated them into this pasta dish. Before serving, I sprinkle bacon crumbs over the spaghetti, which sends the dish over the top.

Serves: **4**   Prep Time: **14 minutes**   Cook Time: **26 minutes**

6 tablespoons olive oil

½ cup finely chopped red bell pepper

½ cup finely chopped onion

½ teaspoon crushed red pepper flakes, or to taste

2 garlic cloves, smashed

½ cup dry white wine or water

24 Manila or littleneck clams, scrubbed

1 12-ounce box gluten-free spaghetti

¼ cup finely chopped fresh parsley, plus more for serving

½ cup finely crushed gluten-free rice cereal, such as Erewhon, or gluten-free bread crumbs

3 slices bacon, cooked until crisp and crumbled

Lemon wedges, for serving

1. Bring a large pot of generously salted water to a boil.
2. In a large saucepan, heat the oil over medium heat. Add the bell pepper, onion and red pepper flakes and cook, stirring, until softened, about 8 minutes. Add the garlic and cook until fragrant, about 2 minutes. Add the wine and cook, uncovered, until the alcohol evaporates, about 3 minutes. Add the clams, shaking the pot gently. Cover and let the clams cook until opened, about 5 minutes. If any have not opened, cook a little longer. If they still do not open, discard them. Remove the saucepan from the heat.
3. Add the spaghetti to the boiling water and cook, stirring occasionally, for 6 minutes; it will still be firm. Drain. Add the spaghetti and parsley to the clams in the saucepan and gently toss. Cook over medium-low heat until the spaghetti is al dente, about 2 minutes more.
4. Chop together the cereal crumbs and bacon. To serve, sprinkle the spaghetti and clams with the bacon crumbs and top with a squeeze of lemon.

EGGPLANT LASAGNA WITH BÉCHAMEL SAUCE

Gluten-free no-boil lasagna sheets are a huge timesaver. There are several brands, but my hands-down favorite is the brown rice lasagna from Jovial. My mom always used unseasoned crushed canned tomatoes as the sauce, which lets the other flavors come through, but you can also use store-bought tomato sauce for a more robust flavor.

Serves: **8 to 10**   Prep Time: **28 minutes**   Cook Time: **55 minutes**

Canola oil or olive oil, for frying

1 cup My Gluten-Free All-Purpose Flour (page 195)

Salt and black pepper

2 medium eggplants (about 2 pounds), sliced into ¼-inch-thick rounds

1 28-ounce can (3 cups) crushed tomatoes

1 9-ounce package gluten-free brown rice no-boil lasagna sheets, or Gluten-Free Fresh Egg Pasta (page 111), rolled out and edges trimmed

1 cup loosely packed chopped fresh basil

1½ cups shredded dairy-free mozzarella-style cheese (optional)

¾ cup Dairy-Free Ricotta Cheese (page 215) or store-bought

3 cups (double batch) Dairy-Free Béchamel (page 210)

1 cup Dairy-Free Grated Parmesan (page 217) or store-bought

1. Preheat the oven to 350°F.
2. Heat the oil, about 1 inch deep, in a large skillet over medium heat until just smoking or until an instant-read thermometer registers 375°F. In a large resealable bag, combine the flour, 2 teaspoons salt and 1 teaspoon pepper. Add the eggplants, seal and shake to coat. Remove the eggplants, shaking off the excess flour. In batches, add the eggplants to the hot oil and fry, turning once, until golden brown, about 2 minutes on each side. Transfer the eggplants to paper towels to drain.
3. Coat the bottom of a 9-by-12-inch baking dish with 1 cup of the tomatoes and cover with 4 lasagna sheets. Build a layer of tomatoes, eggplants, basil, mozzarella, ricotta, béchamel, Parmesan and lasagna sheets, gently pressing down during assembly. Repeat, making one more layer in the same way. Finish the lasagna with a layer of the remaining tomatoes, eggplants, basil, béchamel, and Parmesan.
4. Cover with foil and bake about 30 minutes. Uncover and bake until golden and bubbly, about 10 minutes more. Let sit for 10 minutes before serving.

BEEF NOODLE CASSEROLE

This homey casserole is great for a potluck or any time I need to make something ahead. It's a creamy version of sloppy joe–style beef stirred into noodles and then topped with cheese. You can't get more comfort food than that. Stir in some Dairy-Free Sour Cream (page 211) in place of the cream for a little tang.

Serves: **6 to 8**   Prep Time: **12 minutes**   Cook Time: **45 minutes**

2 tablespoons olive oil, plus more for drizzling

2 carrots, peeled and chopped

1 small onion, chopped

1 green bell pepper, chopped

2 garlic cloves, finely chopped

1 pound ground beef

   Salt and black pepper

1 9-ounce box gluten-free egg noodles

1 28-ounce can tomato puree

1 cup homemade dairy-free heavy cream (page 205) or store-bought dairy-free creamer

¼ cup chopped fresh parsley

2 cups dairy-free shredded cheddar-style cheese, for topping

1. Preheat the oven to 375°F. Spray a 9-inch baking dish with cooking spray. Bring a large pot of generously salted water to a boil.

2. Meanwhile, in a large saucepan, heat the olive oil over medium-high heat. Add the carrots, onion, bell pepper and garlic. Cook, stirring, until softened, about 8 minutes. Add the beef and cook, breaking up the meat, until just cooked through, about 7 minutes. Season with about 1½ teaspoons salt and 1 teaspoon pepper.

3. Meanwhile, add the pasta to the boiling water and cook until al dente; drain.

4. Add the tomato puree to the beef mixture and bring to a boil over medium heat. Stir in the cream and season with about 1½ teaspoons salt. Stir in the cooked noodles and parsley. Transfer the noodle mixture to the dish and scatter the cheese over the top. *(The casserole can be covered and refrigerated overnight. Let return to room temperature before baking.)*

5. Bake, uncovered, until bubbling and heated through, about 25 minutes.

6. Preheat the broiler. Place the casserole under the broiler and broil until golden, 3 to 5 minutes. Let stand for 10 minutes before serving.

BAKED HAM-AND-CHEESE MANICOTTI

Whether you call it manicotti, cannelloni or simply baked pasta, this comforting dish will warm you up any cold winter evening. I fill cooked pasta sheets with ham and dairy-free ricotta, top with a light tomato sauce and bake until nice and bubbly.

Serves: **4 (12 manicotti)** · Prep Time: **24 minutes** · Cook Time: **57 minutes**

2 tablespoons olive oil, plus more for brushing

½ large onion, chopped

1 celery stalk, chopped

1 carrot, peeled and chopped

2 garlic cloves, smashed

3 cups tomato puree

6 tablespoons chopped fresh parsley, plus more for sprinkling

Salt and black pepper

4 cups (double batch) Dairy-Free Ricotta Cheese (page 215) or store-bought, drained

2 large eggs, lightly beaten

¼ pound boiled ham, coarsely chopped

½ teaspoon ground nutmeg

1 recipe Gluten-Free Fresh Egg Pasta (page 111), cut into twelve 4-by-6-inch rectangular pasta sheets or one 8-ounce box store-bought gluten-free large-shell manicotti

1 cup shredded dairy-free mozzarella-style cheese

1. In a large skillet, heat the oil over medium-high heat. Add the onion, celery, carrot and garlic and cook until tender, about 6 minutes. Add the tomato puree and 4 tablespoons of the parsley and bring to a boil. Reduce the heat to medium-low and simmer for 30 minutes. Season with about 1½ teaspoons salt and ½ teaspoon pepper. Remove the garlic. (*The tomato sauce can be covered and refrigerated for up to 1 day.*)

2. Bring a large pot of generously salted water to a boil. Preheat the oven to 425°F. Spray a 9-by-13-inch baking dish with cooking spray.

3. Meanwhile, in a medium bowl, beat the ricotta until creamy. Stir in the eggs, ham, nutmeg, remaining 2 tablespoons parsley, ½ teaspoon salt and ¼ teaspoon pepper. Refrigerate the filling.

4. Working in batches, add the pasta sheets to the boiling water, gently stirring, and cook until the pasta rises to the surface, about 1 minute. Rinse under cold water, drain and pat dry.

5. Spread ½ cup of the tomato sauce in the baking dish. Arrange 1 pasta sheet on a clean work surface and spread about ¼ cup filling across the center. Roll up and place seam side down in the baking dish. Repeat with the remaining pasta and filling, adding the rolls in a single

layer. Top with the remaining tomato sauce, sprinkle with some more parsley and sprinkle with the mozzarella. Tightly cover with foil and bake until heated through and bubbly, about 20 minutes.

6.   Preheat the broiler. Uncover the manicotti, brush the manicotti edges with oil and broil until golden and bubbly, 3 to 5 minutes. Let sit for 5 minutes before serving.

GLUTEN-FREE FRESH EGG PASTA

This handmade pasta recipe is more time-consuming than store-bought, but the process itself is simple, especially after a little practice. The key is patience. Once you get comfortable, go ahead and swap in a ½ cup of another gluten-free flour, like millet or almond, for ½ cup of the all-purpose.

Makes: **About 1 pound**   Prep Time: **30 minutes**

2½ cups My Gluten-Free All-Purpose Flour (page 195), plus more for dusting

½ teaspoon salt

4 large eggs, at room temperature

1½ tablespoons olive oil

2 tablespoons water

1. In the bowl of a stand mixer or in a large bowl with a wooden spoon, blend together the flour and salt. Mix in the eggs, 1 at a time, until the dough starts to come together. Mix in the oil and water; mix until the dough just forms a ball. Use the palms of your hands to knead the dough until smooth and elastic, about 10 minutes. Cut the dough into 4 pieces and cover with plastic wrap; let rest for 30 minutes.

2. Adjust a pasta machine to the first and widest setting. Lightly flour 1 piece of the dough to prevent it from sticking to the rollers and flatten it to about a ½-inch thickness using a rolling pin. Run the dough through the rollers. Fold the dough in thirds and pass it through the same setting again. Repeat this process 2 times. Run the pasta through the next three narrower settings until about ⅛ inch thick. Repeat with the remaining 3 pieces of pasta dough. (*If you're not using the pasta sheets right away, cover them with a moist paper towel and plastic wrap. The pasta will keep refrigerated, for up to 1 hour.*)

MUSHROOM RAVIOLI WITH CREAMY MUSHROOM RAGU

Ravioli are easier than you may think and there's no better feeling than the pride you get from sitting down at the table with a piping-hot plate of pasta that you made with your own hands. Plus, you can stuff the pasta dough with your favorite fillings. I love the earthiness that mushrooms bring, so I add them to both the filling and the sauce.

Serves: 4 (16 large ravioli) · **Prep Time: 30 minutes (plus drying)** · **Cook Time: 23 minute**

2 tablespoons olive oil

2 garlic cloves, finely chopped

3 10-ounce containers button mushrooms, sliced

Salt and black pepper

¼ cup dry white wine

1 large egg, lightly beaten

¼ cup finely crushed gluten-free rice cereal, such as Erewhon

¼ cup finely chopped fresh parsley, plus more for sprinkling

1 recipe Gluten-Free Fresh Egg Pasta (page 111)

1 cup Homemade Cashew or Almond Milk (page 205 or 206) or store-bought dairy-free creamer

1 teaspoon white truffle oil (optional)

Chopped hazelnuts, toasted, for sprinkling

1. In a large skillet, heat the oil over medium heat. Add the garlic and cook, stirring, until fragrant, about 1 minute. Stir in the mushrooms and cook until the mushrooms give up their liquid and the liquid evaporates, about 5 minutes. Season with about 2 teaspoons salt and ½ teaspoon pepper. Add the wine and cook, stirring, until the liquid has evaporated, about 12 minutes. Transfer two thirds of the mushrooms to a bowl. When cool enough to handle, finely chop and return to the bowl. Stir in the egg, cereal crumbs and parsley.

2. On a lightly floured surface, lay out a long sheet of pasta. Leaving a ½-inch border, place four 1-tablespoon portions of the cooled filling about 2 inches apart along the top half of the sheet. Brush the border and in between the filling with water. Fold the bottom half of the dough over the filling to cover, pressing out any air around the filling. Using a fluted pastry cutter or a sharp knife, cut between the mounds to form squares and separate the ravioli. Repeat with the remaining dough and filling. Let the ravioli air-dry on flour-dusted parchment paper or dish towels for about 1 hour. (*The uncooked ravioli can be frozen for up to 1 month. Freeze*

*in a single layer on a baking sheet, then transfer to a large resealable freezer bag. When
ready to use, cook frozen.)*

3. Bring a large pot of generously salted water to a boil. Add the ravioli and cook until they
   float to the top, about 10 minutes. Reserve about ½ cup of the pasta cooking water.

4. Meanwhile, add the milk to the skillet containing the remaining one third of the mushrooms. Cover and heat over medium heat until warmed through; season with salt.

5. Drain the ravioli and transfer to the skillet, adding pasta cooking water if the sauce seems
   dry. Stir in the truffle oil, if using, and sprinkle with hazelnuts and more parsley and serve.

HOMEMADE FETTUCCINE WITH SAUSAGE, BROCCOLI RABE AND PARMESAN

Pasta cooking water helps pull this sauce together. Since it has starch in it from cooking the pasta, it gives the sauce some body, which helps it cling to the pasta. In this recipe, I like to use almond flour, which adds not only moisture and tenderness to the dough, but a sweet nuttiness.

Serves: **4**   Prep Time: **28 minutes**   Cook Time: **10 minutes**

FOR THE PASTA

2½ cups My Gluten-Free All-Purpose Flour (page 195), plus more for dusting

½ cup blanched almond flour, such as Honeyville

½ teaspoon salt

4 large eggs, at room temperature

1 tablespoon olive oil

FOR THE SAUCE

¼ cup olive oil

½ pound sweet Italian pork sausage meat

3 garlic cloves, finely chopped

½ teaspoon crushed red pepper flakes, or to taste

2 cups chopped broccoli rabe

Salt

¼ cup finely chopped fresh parsley

Dairy-Free Grated Parmesan (page 217) or store-bought, for serving

1. **Make the pasta**: In the bowl of a stand mixer or in a large bowl with a wooden spoon, stir together the all-purpose flour, almond flour and salt. Mix in the eggs, one at a time, until the dough starts to come together. Add the oil and mix until the dough just forms a ball. Using the palms of your hands, knead the dough until smooth and elastic, about 3 minutes. Cut the dough into 4 pieces and wrap each with plastic wrap. Let rest for 30 minutes.

2. Adjust a pasta machine to the first and widest setting. Lightly flour 1 piece of the dough to prevent it from sticking to the rollers and flatten to about a ½-inch thickness using a rolling pin. Run the dough through the rollers. Fold the dough in thirds and pass it through the same setting again. Repeat this process 2 times. Run the pasta through the next three narrower settings until about ⅛ inch thick.

3. Using the pasta cutter attachment, cut the pasta sheet lengthwise into fettuccine. Place on a parchment-lined baking sheet. Repeat with the remaining pasta dough. *(The pasta can be frozen on the baking sheet, then transferred to a large resealable freezer bag and frozen for up to 1 month.)*

4. **Make the sauce**: Bring a large pot of generously salted water to boil. Meanwhile, heat the oil in a large saucepan over medium heat. Add the sausage and cook, breaking up the meat, until cooked through, about 5 minutes. Add the garlic, red pepper and broccoli rabe. Season with about ¾ teaspoon salt and cook until just tender, about 3 minutes.

5. Add the pasta to the boiling water and cook until it rises to the surface, about 3 minutes. Reserve 1 cup of the pasta cooking water. Using tongs, transfer the pasta to the sauce along with the parsley. Toss to combine, adding enough pasta cooking water to make a thin sauce that coats the pasta. Divide among shallow bowls, top with Parmesan and serve immediately.

SWEET ALMOND-RAISIN RICE PILAF

The sweetness of almonds, raisins and cinnamon combines with pungent garlic and onion in this rice pilaf. The combination is unexpected and completely satisfying.

Serves: **4**   Prep Time: **8 minutes**   Cook Time: **37 minutes**

3 tablespoons olive oil

½ cup sliced, slivered or chopped almonds

1 small onion, finely chopped

2 garlic cloves, mashed

1 cup long-grain brown or white basmati rice, well rinsed in cold water

Salt and black pepper

½ cup freshly squeezed orange juice (from about 2 oranges)

1½ cups hot water

½ cup golden raisins, dark raisins or dried currants

¼ teaspoon ground cinnamon (optional)

1. Heat 1 tablespoon of the oil in a 2-quart saucepan over medium heat. Add the almonds and toast, shaking the pan occasionally, until golden, about 3 minutes; transfer to a plate.

2. In the same saucepan, heat the remaining 2 tablespoons oil over medium heat. Add the onion and garlic and cook, stirring occasionally, until lightly golden and softened, about 5 minutes. Add the rice and about ¾ teaspoon salt and ⅛ teaspoon pepper; cook, stirring, about 2 minutes. Stir in the orange juice and hot water and bring to a boil. Stir in the raisins and cinnamon and reduce the heat to medium-low. Cover and cook for 30 minutes. Turn off the heat and let stand, covered, for 5 minutes. Fluff with a fork and stir in the almonds. Serve hot or at room temperature. (*The rice can be made 1 day ahead and chilled. Reheat, covered, in a 250°F oven until heated through, about 30 minutes.*)

SPANAKOPITA RICE

I fold the flavors of the classic Greek appetizer, spanakopita, into this rice dish. For the perfect finish, I top the spinach, dill and parsley–flecked rice with yogurt, olives, lemon and sesame seeds.

Serves: **4**   Prep Time: **10 minutes**   Cook Time: **32 minutes**

¼ cup olive oil

1 onion, chopped

2 scallions, thinly sliced crosswise

1 cup long-grain white rice, well rinsed in cold water

2 cups water

1¼ teaspoons salt

¼ teaspoon black pepper

1 10-ounce package frozen chopped spinach, thawed and squeezed dry

¼ cup finely chopped fresh dill

¼ cup finely chopped fresh parsley

Dairy-Free Traditional Yogurt (page 213) or store-bought, chopped kalamata olives and lemon wedges, for serving

2 teaspoons sesame seeds, toasted

1. Heat the oil in a 2-quart saucepan over medium heat. Add the onion and scallions and cook, stirring occasionally, until lightly golden and softened, about 5 minutes.

2. Add the rice, water, salt and pepper. Cover and simmer over low heat for 10 minutes. Scatter the spinach, dill and parsley over the rice. Cover and cook until the rice is tender, about 10 minutes more. Remove from the heat and let stand, covered, for 5 minutes.

3. Fluff the rice with a fork. To serve, top each serving with a dollop of yogurt, olives and a squeeze of lemon. Sprinkle with the sesame seeds and serve.

SHRIMP FRIED RICE

When I was growing up, we lived for five years outside San Francisco, home to some of the best Chinese restaurants in America. So I have high expectations for fried rice. This one is as good as any Chinatown version.

For best results, use day-old rice. The finished dish freezes beautifully: Just place cooled fried rice in a freezer-friendly container. Defrost overnight in the fridge or just heat in the microwave.

Serves: 4   **Prep Time: 12 minutes**   **Cook Time: 18 minutes**

3 tablespoons gluten-free tamari

2¼ teaspoons gluten-free hoisin sauce

2¼ teaspoons rice wine vinegar

1½ teaspoons sesame oil

⅛ teaspoon sugar

3 tablespoons canola oil

2 large eggs, lightly beaten

  Salt and black pepper

½ pound medium shrimp, peeled, deveined and tails discarded

½ teaspoon cornstarch

1 small onion, chopped

3 scallions, chopped crosswise

4 cups cooked long-grain white rice, at room temperature (from 2 cups uncooked rice)

½ cup frozen peas, thawed

1. In a small bowl, whisk together the tamari, hoisin sauce, vinegar, sesame oil and sugar.

2. Heat 1 tablespoon of the canola oil in a large skillet over high heat until hot, but not smoking. Add the eggs and season with salt and pepper. Scramble until fluffy and just cooked through, about 1 minute. Transfer to a plate. Wipe out the skillet with a paper towel.

3. In a small bowl, toss together the shrimp and cornstarch. Heat 1 tablespoon of the canola oil in the skillet over high heat. Add the shrimp and season with ¼ teaspoon salt and ⅛ teaspoon pepper. Cook, turning once, for 1 minute, or until cooked through. Transfer to a plate.
   Wipe out the skillet with a paper towel.

4. Heat the remaining 1 tablespoon canola oil in the skillet over medium heat. Add the onion and scallions and cook, stirring, until fragrant, about 3 minutes. Fold in the rice, breaking up any clumps, and cook until heated through and lightly browned, about 10 minutes. Return the shrimp and egg to the skillet, along with the peas and tamari mixture. Toss everything together to heat through, about 3 minutes, and serve.

ONE-POT CHICKEN-PARM RICE

Who doesn't love a good chicken Parmesan? This casserole version is healthier than the old-school version but still delivers a serious serving of hominess.

Serves: **4**   Prep Time: **8 minutes**   Cook Time: **55 minutes**

2 tablespoons olive oil

3 garlic cloves, smashed

4 boneless, skinless chicken breasts, pounded thin

Salt and black pepper

½ cup My Gluten-Free All-Purpose Flour (page 195)

1 cup long-grain white rice, well rinsed in cold water

1 14.5-ounce can chopped tomatoes (about 1½ cups)

1 cup homemade or store-bought chicken broth or water

1 8-ounce can tomato sauce (about 1 cup)

6 large fresh basil leaves, torn

¼ cup Dairy-Free Grated Parmesan (page 217) or store-bought

1 cup shredded dairy-free mozzarella-style cheese, for topping

1. In a large Dutch oven, heat the oil over medium-high heat. Add the garlic and cook until golden, about 1 minute. Meanwhile, season the chicken generously with salt and pepper and lightly dredge in the flour. Working with 2 pieces at a time, add the chicken to the Dutch oven and cook, turning once, until browned, about 4 minutes total. Transfer to a platter.

2. Add the rice to the Dutch oven and stir to coat, about 2 minutes. Add the tomatoes, broth and 2 teaspoons salt. Bring to a boil. Top with the chicken, tomato sauce, basil, Parmesan and mozzarella. Cover, reduce the heat to low and gently simmer until the chicken and rice are cooked, 30 to 40 minutes. Serve hot.

Fake-Out Takeout, TV Dinners
and Restaurant Classics

MEAL MAKEOVERS

Going gluten-free means that it can be tricky to go out to restaurants, order takeout for delivery or grab your favorite TV dinner from the freezer section of your supermarket. These recipes make putting dinner on the table easy. My kids and I like to choose from our repetoire of reclaimed restaurant favorites for our themed dinners, like Tex-Mex, Italian, Chinese and barbecue.

MUSHROOM VEGGIE BURGERS

If I'm going to eat a veggie burger, it's got to taste meaty and that means mushrooms. These are inspired by Amy's Cheddar Veggie Burgers. The trick was getting the texture right, which I did with a combination of brown rice, walnuts, oats and potato flakes, all of which help bind together the ingredients.

Sometimes, if I want a more uniform texture, I place the veggie burger mixture in my food processor and pulse a few times. Hungry for more than mushrooms? Swap in 1 cup drained caponata (page 104) for the sautéed mushroom mixture.

Makes: **4 burgers**   Prep Time: **15 minutes**   Cook Time: **22 minutes**

2 tablespoons olive oil

½ small onion, finely chopped

1 10-ounce container button mushrooms, stemmed and finely chopped

1 carrot, peeled and finely chopped

1 celery stalk, finely chopped

1 cup cooked brown rice (from ½ cup uncooked rice)

½ cup gluten-free old-fashioned rolled oats

½ cup chopped walnuts

2 tablespoons My Gluten-Free All-Purpose Flour (page 195)

2 tablespoons potato flakes

½ teaspoon salt

4 store-bought gluten-free hamburger buns, split and toasted

Shredded iceberg lettuce, tomato slices, thinly sliced red onion, pickle chips, ketchup and mustard, for serving

1. In a large skillet, heat 1 tablespoon of the oil over medium heat. Add the onion and cook, stirring, until softened, about 5 minutes. Add the mushrooms, carrot and celery and cook until the liquid from the mushrooms has evaporated, about 10 minutes.

2. Transfer to a large bowl and let cool. Stir the rice, oats, walnuts, flour, potato flakes and salt into the bowl. If necessary, add water, 1 tablespoon at a time, until combined.

3. Shape the mixture into 4 patties. Wipe out the skillet and heat the remaining 1 tablespoon oil in a large skillet over medium-high heat. Add the patties and cook until golden on the bottoms, about 5 minutes. Flip and cook until golden on the other side, about 2 minutes more. Place the burgers on buns and serve with condiments of choice.

MOO SHU VEGETABLES WITH SESAME PANCAKES

If you don't want to make the pancakes, you can use Bibb lettuce leaves, rice paper wrappers or gluten-free tortillas instead. To add protein, stir in chopped plain or smoked firm tofu, scrambled eggs, cooked shrimp or thin strips of beef, pork or chicken.

Serves: **4 to 6 (6 pancakes)**   Prep Time: **20 minutes (plus resting)**   Cook Time: **15 minutes**

FOR THE VEGETABLES

- 2 tablespoons olive oil or unflavored coconut oil
- 2 garlic cloves, finely chopped
- 1 tablespoon finely chopped peeled fresh ginger
- 2 3.5-ounce packages shiitake mushrooms, stemmed and thinly sliced
- 3 cups shredded cabbage
- 1½ cups snow peas, thinly sliced lengthwise
- 3 large carrots, peeled and shredded
- 1½ teaspoons salt
- ½ teaspoon black pepper
- 2 tablespoons gluten-free hoisin sauce, plus more for serving

FOR THE PANCAKES

- 2 cups My Gluten-Free All-Purpose Flour (page 195)
- 1 teaspoon salt
- 1 cup boiling water
- Sesame oil, for brushing

1. **Make the vegetables**: Heat the oil in a large skillet over medium-high heat. Add the garlic, ginger and mushrooms and cook, stirring, until the mushrooms begin to soften, about 5 minutes. Stir in the cabbage, snow peas, carrots, salt and pepper and cook until just wilted, about 4 minutes. Stir in the hoisin sauce until combined. Keep warm.

2. **Make the pancakes**: Place the flour in a large bowl. Add the salt and gradually stir in the boiling water until a dough forms. Using a wooden spoon, beat until the dough pulls away from the sides of the bowl, about 2 minutes. Divide the dough into 2 equal pieces and cover 1 piece tightly with plastic wrap.

3. Place 1 dough piece on a lightly floured 12-inch-long piece of parchment paper. Lightly flour the top and, using a rolling pin, roll the dough out until about ¼ inch thick. Cut into 12 rounds with a 3-inch cutter. Brush a bit of sesame oil on 6 of the rounds, top with the remaining rounds and press together. Roll each into a 7-inch circle to make 6 pancakes. Cover loosely with plastic wrap. Let the pancakes rest at room temperature for about 30 minutes.

4. Heat a large cast-iron skillet over medium-high heat. Add 1 pancake and cook, flipping once, until cooked through but still flexible, about 1 minute on each side. Repeat with the remaining pancakes. *(The pancakes can be stacked, wrapped in foil and kept warm in a 200°F oven until ready to serve.)*

5. To serve, place a pancake on a plate, spread on a little hoisin sauce, top with some sautéed vegetables and roll up, burrito-style.

RANCH CHICKEN NUGGETS

I was growing tired of the same old chicken nuggets so I decided to experiment with different flavor combinations. My favorite was this riff on chicken Cordon Bleu, ham rolled around chicken with a creamy surprise inside. Instead of Gruyère cheese, I use homemade ranch dressing to keep the chicken juicy and the filling rich.

Serves: **4**   Prep Time: **18 minutes**   Cook Time: **25 minutes**

½ cup My Gluten-Free All-Purpose Flour (page 195)

2 large eggs, beaten with 1 tablespoon water

1 cup finely crushed gluten-free rice cereal, such as Erewhon

¾ teaspoon salt

¼ teaspoon black pepper

6 slices cooked deli ham (about ½ pound), cut lengthwise into 1-inch-wide strips

½ cup Dairy-Free Ranch Dressing (page 223) or store-bought

2 large boneless, skinless chicken breasts (about 1 pound), cut into 1-inch-wide pieces

1. Preheat the oven to 350°F. Set two wire racks over two baking sheets and spray with cooking spray.
2. Place the flour on a plate and the egg mixture in a shallow bowl. Combine the cereal crumbs, salt and pepper on another plate.
3. Place the ham strips on a work surface and put a dollop of ranch dressing at the bottom of each strip. Top with a piece of chicken and roll up to enclose. Lightly coat each rolled-up chicken piece with the flour, then egg, then cereal crumbs. Place, seam side down, on the racks.
4. Lightly spray the nuggets with cooking spray. Bake until crisp and cooked through, about 25 minutes. Serve hot.

CRISPY FRIED CHICKEN

Coconut milk is not the first ingredient that comes to mind when marinating chicken for frying. But much like regular buttermilk, it yields meat that's moist and tender. If you're not big on coconut-scented chicken, don't worry, you'll barely taste it.

No deep-fry thermometer? Test if your oil is hot enough by adding a pinch of gluten-free flour to the oil. If it sizzles and rises to the surface, you're ready to start frying. The chicken is fully cooked when an instant-read thermometer inserted near the bone measures 170°F.

Serves: **4**   Prep Time: **18 minutes (plus marinating)**   Cook Time: **20 minutes**

1   13-ounce can full-fat coconut milk

2   large eggs, at room temperature

1   tablespoon chili powder

1   teaspoon salt

¼   teaspoon black pepper

1   3½-pound chicken, cut into 8 pieces, or 3½ pounds chicken pieces, patted dry

1½   cups My Gluten-Free All-Purpose Flour (page 195)

¼   cup cornstarch

2   tablespoons Old Bay seasoning

1   teaspoon baking powder

    Canola oil, for frying

1. In a large bowl, whisk together the milk, eggs, chili powder, salt and pepper. Add the chicken, cover and refrigerate for at least 1 hour or overnight. Line a baking sheet with parchment paper.

2. In a shallow bowl, whisk together the flour, cornstarch, Old Bay and baking powder. Drain the chicken and dredge in the flour mixture. Place on the baking sheet.

3. In a large cast-iron skillet, heat 1 inch of oil over medium heat until a deep-fry thermometer measures 360°F.

4. Carefully add the chicken to the hot oil and fry, turning occasionally, until cooked through, about 20 minutes; drain on a paper towel–lined wire rack. (*The fried chicken can be kept warm in a 250°F oven for up to 1 hour or served at room temperature.*)

CHICKEN POTPIE POPPERS

Growing up in an Italian-American household and eating at Italian trattorias, I've had my fair share of stuffed rice balls. I was trying to come up with a similar dish, and I also wanted to make a meal out of them. Enter the chicken potpie popper. With each bite, you get a mouthful of the best part of potpie—the creamy chicken-mushroom mixture. For creaminess, I use mayonnaise, which I've found to be the key to maintaining moistness.

Serves: **4 to 6**   Prep Time: **20 minutes**   Cook Time: **15 minutes**

2 tablespoons olive oil

¼ cup finely chopped onion

¼ cup finely chopped celery

¼ cup finely chopped carrot

¼ cup frozen peas

1 cup thinly sliced mushrooms

2½ cups shredded cooked chicken

3 cups finely crushed gluten-free rice cereal, such as Erewhon

¼ cup finely chopped fresh parsley

1 teaspoon chopped fresh thyme leaves

½ teaspoon salt

¼ teaspoon black pepper

½ cup Dairy-Free Mayonnaise (pag 221) or store-bought

4 large eggs

Vegetable oil, for frying

1. Heat the oil in a medium skillet over medium-high heat. Add the onion, celery, carrot, peas and mushrooms and cook, stirring, until softened, about 5 minutes.

2. In a large bowl, combine the onion mixture with the chicken, 1½ cups of the cereal crumbs, parsley, thyme, salt and pepper; let cool. Stir in the mayonnaise and 2 of the eggs until combined. Form into 2-inch ovals and place on a parchment-lined baking sheet. Refrigerate for 10 minutes.

3. Heat about 1 inch vegetable oil in a large pot over medium heat until a deep-fry thermometer measures 375°F.

4. Meanwhile, place the remaining 1½ cups cereal crumbs in a shallow bowl. In another shallow bowl, beat the remaining 2 eggs. Coat a chicken popper with the cereal crumbs, dip into the eggs, then coat again with the cereal crumbs; return to the baking sheet. Repeat with the remaining chicken poppers.

5. In batches, add the poppers to the hot oil and fry, turning occasionally, until golden brown, about 2 minutes. Return the oil to 375°F between batches. Remove with a slotted spoon and drain on paper towels. Serve hot.

VARIATION

BAKED CHICKEN POTPIE POPPERS: Preheat the oven to 425°F. Place the coated poppers on a lightly greased baking sheet. Bake, turning the poppers halfway through, until crunchy and golden, about 20 minutes.

CREAMY CHICKEN DIVAN CASSEROLE

A TV dinner classic, chicken divan—chicken and broccoli in a cream sauce—is easily one of my all-time favorite frozen meals. I like this recipe because the slow cooker does most of the work.

Serves: **4 to 6**   Prep Time: **16 minutes**   Cook Time: **2½ hours**

3 tablespoons olive oil

1 small onion, finely chopped

2 celery stalks, halved lengthwise and cut into ¼-inch pieces

2 garlic cloves, chopped

1 tablespoon chopped fresh thyme

1 teaspoon paprika

Salt and black pepper

¼ cup My Gluten-Free All-Purpose Flour (page 195)

1½ cups homemade or store-bought chicken broth

½ cup homemade dairy-free heavy cream (page 205) or store-bought dairy-free creamer

1 tablespoon plus 1½ teaspoons Dijon mustard

4 boneless, skinless chicken breasts (1½–2 pounds), cut into 2-inch pieces

2 cups instant rice

2 10-ounce packages frozen broccoli florets, thawed

½ cup finely crushed gluten-free rice cereal, such as Erewhon

1. In a large skillet, heat 2 tablespoons of the oil over medium heat. Add the onion, celery, garlic, thyme, paprika, ¾ teaspoon salt and ¼ teaspoon pepper. Cook, stirring, until the onion is softened, about 5 minutes. Sprinkle the flour on top; stir for 1 minute. Remove from the heat and gradually stir in the broth, cream and 1 tablespoon of the mustard. Transfer the cream sauce to a slow cooker.

2. Generously season the chicken all over with salt and pepper and stir into the cream sauce to coat. Cover and cook on high for 2 hours. Stir in the rice and 1 teaspoon salt and cook for 10 minutes. Stir in the broccoli and cook until the chicken is cooked through and the rice is tender, about 10 minutes.

3. Meanwhile, in a small bowl, combine the cereal crumbs, remaining 1½ teaspoons mustard and ¼ teaspoon salt. In a small skillet, heat the remaining 1 tablespoon oil over medium heat. Add the crumb mixture and toast, about 1 minute. Scatter the mustard crumbs over the chicken and serve.

BAKED CHICKEN DIVAN CASSEROLE: Stir together the cream sauce, seasoned uncooked chicken, broccoli, rice and 1 teaspoon salt and place in a 9-by-13-inch baking dish. Cover tightly with foil and bake in a 350°F oven until the chicken is cooked through and the rice is tender, 50 to 60 minutes. Remove the foil, top with the mustard crumbs and bake for 15 minutes more. Let cool for about 10 minutes before serving.

SWEET-AND-SOUR CHICKEN

This sauce, with the perfect balance of sweet and sour, combines pineapple juice and chunks with rice wine vinegar and, surprisingly, ketchup. The batter for the chicken contains seltzer—a trick I learned from my Italian grandfather, which makes for a crispy coating.

Serves: **4**   Prep Time: **18 minutes**   Cook Time: **35 minutes**

1½ cups My Gluten-Free All-Purpose Flour (page 195)

½ cup finely crushed gluten-free rice cereal, such as Erewhon

1½ teaspoons baking powder

½ teaspoon salt

1½ cups seltzer

2 large egg whites, beaten

1 tablespoon canola oil, plus more for frying

4 red bell peppers, cut into 1-inch pieces

2 cups canned pineapple chunks, drained, 1 cup juice reserved

1½ cups homemade or store-bought chicken broth or water

3 tablespoons ketchup

3 tablespoons rice wine vinegar

2 tablespoons gluten-free tamari

2 tablespoons sugar

1½ teaspoons cornstarch dissolved in 1½ tablespoons water

1 pound boneless, skinless chicken breasts, cut into 1-inch pieces

1. In a food processor, combine 1 cup of the flour, the cereal crumbs, baking powder and salt. Add the seltzer and egg whites and whisk until smooth. Cover and refrigerate for 15 minutes.

2. In a large nonstick skillet, heat the 1 tablespoon oil over medium-high heat. Add the bell peppers and cook until slightly softened, about 2 minutes. Add the pineapple, pineapple juice, broth, ketchup, vinegar, tamari and sugar. Lower the heat to medium-low and cook, stirring occasionally, until reduced, about 20 minutes. Stir in the cornstarch mixture and cook until thickened, about 1 minute. Remove the sweet-and-sour sauce from the heat, cover and keep warm.

3. Meanwhile, heat 1 inch oil in a large pot over medium-high heat until a deep-fry thermometer measures 350°F.

4. Place the remaining ½ cup flour in a shallow dish. Working in batches, lightly dredge the chicken pieces in the flour, then coat with the cereal-crumb batter. Add to the hot oil in batches and fry, turning once, until golden brown and the internal temperature measures 165°F on an instant-read thermometer, about 4 minutes total. Return the oil to 165°F between batches. Remove with a slotted spoon and drain on paper towels; season with salt. Transfer the chicken pieces to a platter and serve hot with the sweet- and-sour sauce.

TURKEY CHILI TACO MINI BOWLS

Taco bowls are cup-shaped tortillas filled with a turkey chili flavored with two of my favorite pantry ingredients—peanuts and chocolate. The result is reminiscent of Mexican mole.

Serves: **4**   Prep Time: **10 minutes**   Cook Time: **37 minutes**

- 8 6-inch store-bought gluten-free flour or corn tortillas
- 2 tablespoons olive oil
- ½ onion, finely chopped
  Salt and black pepper
- 1 pound ground turkey
- 2 teaspoons chili powder
- 1 teaspoon ground cumin
- 1 28-ounce can chopped tomatoes
- 1 15-ounce can black beans, rinsed and drained
- 1 cup peanuts or slivered almonds
- ½ ounce (about 2 tablespoons) dairy-free semisweet chocolate chips
  Dairy-Free Sour Cream (page 211) or store-bought, sliced jalapeños, sliced radishes and fresh cilantro or parsley, for topping

1. Preheat the oven to 375°F. Invert a muffin pan and lightly grease the back of eight muffin cups with cooking spray.
2. Meanwhile, stack the tortillas on a microwave-safe plate, cover and microwave on high until softened, about 30 seconds.
3. Drape the softened tortillas over the greased muffin cups to cover. Bake until golden, about 5 minutes. Let cool slightly, then remove the taco bowls from the muffin pan and invert onto a baking sheet to cool completely.
4. Meanwhile, in a large skillet, heat the oil over medium heat. Add the onion, ½ teaspoon salt and ¼ teaspoon pepper and cook, stirring, until softened, about 5 minutes. Add the turkey, raise the heat to medium-high, and cook, breaking up the meat, until cooked through, about 6 minutes. Season with the chili powder, cumin, about 1 tablespoon salt and ½ teaspoon pepper. Stir in the tomatoes and reduce the heat to low. Cover partially and let simmer until thickened, about 15 minutes. Stir in the beans, peanuts and chocolate. Cook until heated through, about 5 minutes.
5. To serve, divide the chili among the taco bowls and scatter the toppings over the chili.

JAMAICAN BEEF PATTIES

After many trips to Montego Bay, Ocho Rios and Negril, I decided it was time to make my own Jamaican patties—yellow-tinted pastries filled with spicy beef. I added rice cereal crumbs to the beef filling to absorb extra moisture so that when you take a bite of the pastry, the patty doesn't all fall apart. The vinegar in the pastry ensures tenderness.

Makes: **Serves 4 (12 patties)**   Prep Time: **18 minutes**   Cook Time: **28 minutes**

FOR THE FILLING

- 1   pound ground beef
- 1   small onion, chopped
- 2   scallions, thinly sliced
- 2   garlic cloves, finely chopped
- 1   jalapeño pepper, seeded and finely chopped
- 2   teaspoons fresh thyme
- 2   teaspoons salt
- 1   teaspoon black pepper
- 1   teaspoon sugar
- ½   teaspoon paprika
- ¼   teaspoon ground allspice
- ½   cup finely crushed gluten-free rice cereal, such as Erewhon
- ½   cup water

FOR THE DOUGH

- 4   cups My Gluten-Free All-Purpose Flour (page 195)
- 2   teaspoons ground turmeric
- 2   teaspoons salt
- 1   teaspoon curry powder
- 1½ cups cold shortening, chopped
- ¾   cup cold water
- 2   teaspoons distilled white vinegar
- 2   large eggs, beaten

1. **Make the filling:** In a large pan over medium heat, cook the beef, breaking it up with a wooden spoon, until browned and crumbly, about 8 minutes. Stir in the onion, scallions, garlic, jalapeño, thyme, salt, pepper, sugar, paprika and allspice. Remove from the heat and stir in the cereal crumbs and water; let cool.

2. **Make the dough:** Preheat the oven to 400°F with a rack in the middle. Line a baking sheet with parchment paper.

3. In a food processor, pulse together the flour, turmeric, salt and curry powder. Add the shortening and process until the mixture resembles

coarse crumbs. In a small bowl, combine the cold water and vinegar and, with the motor running, slowly stream into the dough until a ball forms.

4. On a lightly floured work surface, roll out the dough to about ¼ inch thick. Using a 4½-inch round cookie cutter, cut out 12 circles and transfer to the baking sheet. Brush the edge of one circle with beaten egg. Place about 2 tablespoons filling in the center, fold the circle in half and press the edges together to seal. Use a fork to crimp the edges. Brush the top with the beaten egg. Repeat to make 12 patties.

5. Bake until golden, about 20 minutes. Serve warm or at room temperature.

SAUSAGE FRENCH-BREAD PIZZAS WITH MUSHROOM GRAVY

I love the combination of sausage and mushrooms—especially on pizza. Before serving this French bread pizza, I smother the bread with mushroom gravy.

Makes: **4 French bread pizzas** · Prep Time: **12 minutes** · Cook Time: **25 minutes**

2 tablespoons olive oil

1 pound sweet Italian sausage meat

Salt and black pepper

1 15-ounce can pizza or tomato sauce

1 10-ounce container button mushrooms, stemmed and sliced

1 teaspoon dried oregano

2 tablespoons My Gluten-Free All-Purpose Flour (page 195)

¾ cup homeade or store-bought chicken broth

¼ cup homemade dairy-free heavy cream (page 205) or store-bought dairy-free creamer

1½ teaspoons Dijon mustard

1 loaf French Baguette (page 42) or store-bought gluten-free baguette, split lengthwise, halved and hollowed out slightly

1. Heat 1 tablespoon of the oil in a skillet over medium heat. Add the sausage and cook, breaking up the meat with a wooden spoon, until browned, about 6 minutes; season with salt and pepper. Transfer to a medium bowl and stir in the pizza sauce.

2. In the same skillet, heat the remaining 1 table-spoon oil. Add the mushrooms, oregano, ¾ teaspoon salt and ¼ teaspoon pepper and cook, stirring, until the liquid from the mushrooms has evaporated, about 10 minutes. Sprinkle with the flour and stir for 1 minute. Remove from the heat and gradually stir in the broth, cream and mustard; season with salt. Keep the gravy warm.

3. Preheat the broiler.

4. Lightly toast the French bread halves under the broiler. Fill each bread shell with the sausage mixture. Broil until the bread is crisp, about 3 minutes. Smother each pizza with the mushroom gravy and serve.

DEEP-DISH PIZZA SUPREME

Whether you think of Pizzeria Uno, Pizza Hut, Red Baron or Gino's East, you know what deep-dish pizza means—a thick, chewy crust topped with loads of ingredients. My supreme-style pizza is piled high with pepperoni, Canadian bacon, bell peppers, onions and olives.

Makes: Two 9-inch pizzas   Prep Time: 20 minutes (plus rising)   Cook Time: 25 minutes

1   recipe My Gluten-Free Sandwich Loaf Bread and Pizza Mix (page 197), plus more for dusting

1¾   cups lukewarm water

2   large eggs, at room temperature

8   tablespoons olive oil

½   cup store-bought or homemade pizza sauce

1½   cups shredded dairy-free mozzarella-style cheese

2   ounces Canadian bacon, diced

12   small slices gluten-free pepperoni

½   red bell pepper, thinly sliced

½   green bell pepper, thinly sliced

½   cup thinly sliced red onion

2   tablespoons sliced black olives, drained, for sprinkling

1. Place the bread mix in the bowl of a stand mixer. Using the paddle attachment and with the motor on low speed, add the water, eggs and 2 tablespoons of the oil until combined. Increase the speed to medium and beat for 3 minutes. Divide the dough into 2 equal pieces.

2. Preheat the oven to 400°F with a rack in the middle.

3. Divide the remaining 6 tablespoons olive oil between two 9-inch round cake pans. On a piece of parchment paper lightly dusted with flour, roll each dough piece out to a 9-inch circle. Place in the pans, cover loosely with plastic wrap and let rise at room temperature until doubled in size, about 1½ hours.

4. Dollop each pizza round with half of the sauce, sprinkle with half of the mozzarella and top with half of the toppings.

5. Bake the pizzas until golden and bubbling, about 25 minutes. Let cool slightly. Remove each pizza to a cutting board and, using a pizza cutter or serrated knife, cut into 4 to 6 pieces and serve.

CRISPY FISH STICKS WITH SWEET-RELISH TARTAR SAUCE

I love the combination of crunchy corn flakes, sesame seeds and chili powder in the coating for these fish sticks. You can make a double batch and freeze half of the uncooked fish sticks in a single layer in a resealable bag for up to 1 month. You can also bake them: Place on a baking sheet lined with parchment paper that has been sprayed with cooking spray, spray the fish stick with cooking spray and bake in a preheated 375°F oven, turning once until golden, about 15 minutes.

Serves: **4**   Prep Time: **12 minutes**   Cook Time: **9 minutes**

FOR THE TARTAR SAUCE

- 1 cup Dairy-Free Mayonnaise (page 221) or store-bought
- ¼ cup sweet relish
- 2 tablespoons yellow mustard
- 1 tablespoon fresh lemon juice
- 1 tablespoon finely chopped fresh herbs, such as chives, dill or parsley
- Salt and black pepper

FOR THE FISH STICKS

- 3 cups corn flakes
- 3 tablespoons sesame seeds
- 2 tablespoons chili powder or paprika
- 1 tablespoon sugar
- Salt and black pepper
- ¾ cup Dairy-Free Mayonnaise
- ¼ cup yellow mustard
- Peanut oil or coconut oil, for frying
- 2 pounds halibut or cod fillets, cut into ½-inch-wide strips

1. **Make the tartar sauce:** In a small bowl, stir together the mayonnaise, relish, mustard, lemon juice and herbs. Season with salt and pepper and refrigerate.

2. **Make the fish sticks:** In a food processor, combine the corn flakes, sesame seeds, chili powder, sugar, 1 tablespoon salt and ½ teaspoon pepper. Pulse until coarsely chopped. Transfer to a shallow bowl.

3. In a separate shallow bowl, combine the mayonnaise and mustard.

4. Heat about 1 inch oil in a large pot over medium-high heat until it measures 350°F on a deep-fry thermometer. Preheat the oven to 250°F.

5. Season the fish with salt and pepper. Working in batches, dredge the fish strips in the mayo mixture, then coat completely with the corn flake mixture. Add to the hot oil and fry, turning once, until golden and cooked through, about 3 minutes total. Remove with a slotted spoon and drain on paper towels; season with salt. Keep warm in the oven while you fry the remaining fish sticks. Serve with the tartar sauce.

PRETZEL-CRUSTED MINI CRAB CAKES WITH DIJON DIPPING SAUCE

Instead of using bread crumbs for this restaurant appetizer, I coat the crab cakes with crushed gluten-free pretzels, which add just the right amount of salt. Mayonnaise keeps the crabmeat moist, while Dijon mustard and Worcestershire sauce add zip. If you don't have gluten-free pretzels, use crushed rice cereal, tortilla chips or even potato chips.

Makes: **16 mini crab cakes**   Prep Time: **15 minutes (plus chilling)**   Cook Time: **12 minutes**

FOR THE CRAB CAKES

- 1 pound lump crabmeat, picked over
- ½ cup Dairy-Free Mayonnaise (page 221) or store-bought
- 1 large egg, lightly beaten
- 1½ cups finely ground gluten-free pretzels
- 1 tablespoon Dijon mustard
- ½ teaspoon gluten-free Worcestershire sauce
- 2 tablespoons finely chopped fresh parsley
- Salt
- 4 tablespoons olive oil

FOR THE DIPPING SAUCE

- 1 cup Dairy-Free Mayonnaise
- ½ cup Dijon mustard
- ½ cup whole-grain mustard
- ¼ cup honey
- 1 tablespoon fresh lemon juice
- 1 tablespoon sweet or smoked paprika
- Salt and black pepper

1. **Make the crab cakes:** In a large bowl, combine the crabmeat, mayonnaise, egg, ½ cup of the pretzel crumbs, mustard, Worcestershire sauce, parsley and ¼ teaspoon salt. Shape into 16 cakes about 1 inch thick. Place the remaining 1 cup pretzel crumbs in a shallow bowl. Dredge the cakes in the crumbs and place on a parchment paper–lined baking sheet. Cover and refrigerate until firm, at least 1 hour or overnight.

2. In a large skillet, heat 2 tablespoons of the oil over medium heat. Add half of the crab cakes and cook, turning once, until golden, about 3 minutes on each side. Drain on paper towels. *(You can keep the crab cakes warm in a 250°F oven for about 20 minutes.)* Repeat with the remaining 2 tablespoons oil and crab cakes.

3. **Make the dipping sauce:** In a medium bowl, combine the mayonnaise, mustards, honey, lemon juice and paprika. Season with salt and pepper.

4. Serve the crab cakes with the dipping sauce.

STICKY SESAME SALMON WITH ORANGE SAUCE

My kids are always happy to eat salmon. This recipe is a riff on a dish that we order at our favorite Chinese restaurant in Brooklyn. The sesame seeds coat the surface of the fish, adding a nice nutty crunch. Use the 4 tablespoons sugar if you prefer your sauce on the sweeter side.

Serves: **4**   Prep Time: **8 minutes**   Cook Time: **12 minutes**

FOR THE SAUCE

- ¼ cup ketchup
- ¼ cup orange juice, preferably freshly squeezed
- 2–4 tablespoons sugar
- 2 tablespoons chili paste, such as sambal oelek, or to taste
- 1 tablespoon sesame oil

FOR THE FISH

- 4 6-ounce salmon fillets, skin removed
- Salt and black pepper
- 3 tablespoons olive oil
- ⅓ cup sesame seeds

1. Preheat the oven to 350°F.
2. **Make the sauce:** In a large bowl, stir together the ketchup, orange juice, sugar, chili paste and sesame oil. Set aside.
3. **Make the fish:** Season the salmon generously with salt and pepper, then drizzle with 2 tablespoons of the olive oil. Place the seeds on a plate and dredge the tops of the fillets in the sesame seeds to coat.
4. In an ovenproof skillet, heat the remaining 1 tablespoon olive oil over medium-high heat. Add the salmon, sesame seed side down, to the pan and sear, turning once, until golden brown, about 3 minutes on each side.
5. Transfer the skillet to the oven and roast the salmon until cooked through, about 6 minutes.
6. Generously brush with the orange sauce and serve.

BANG BANG–STYLE SHRIMP

I have my mom to thank for getting me hooked on this popular chain-restaurant dish. The two most important things to figure out in re-creating the dish were the coating for the shrimp and the sweet-and-spicy sauce they are tossed in right before serving. After a few attempts, I settled on a light tempura-like cornstarch batter and a blend of mayo, Thai chili sauce, honey and Sriracha for the sauce.

Serves: **4**   Prep Time: **15 minutes**   Cook Time: **6 minutes**

FOR THE SAUCE

½ cup Dairy-Free Mayonnaise (page 221) or store-bought

⅓ cup gluten-free Thai sweet chili sauce

1¼ teaspoons Sriracha, or to taste

1 teaspoon honey

¼ teaspoon salt

FOR THE SHRIMP

Vegetable oil, for frying

¾ cup My Gluten-Free All-Purpose Flour (page 195)

¾ cup cornstarch

1 teaspoon salt

½ teaspoon black pepper

2 large eggs

1 pound medium shrimp, peeled and deveined

Bibb lettuce leaves, for serving

Thinly sliced scallions, for serving

1. **Make the sauce:** In a small bowl, stir together all the ingredients.
2. **Make the shrimp:** Heat about 2 inches oil in a deep, heavy-bottomed skillet over medium heat until it measures 350°F on a deep-fry thermometer.
3. In a shallow bowl, whisk together the flour, cornstarch, salt and pepper. In another shallow bowl, beat together the eggs.
4. Working in batches, dredge the shrimp in the flour mixture, shake off any excess, dip in the beaten eggs, then dredge again in the flour mixture. Add to the hot oil and fry until golden, turning once, about 2 minutes. Using a slotted spoon, transfer to paper towels to drain. Repeat with the remaining shrimp, returning the oil to 350°F between batches.
5. Toss the shrimp with the chili sauce. Place the lettuce leaves on a serving plate, top with the shrimp, sprinkle with the scallions and serve.

Dessert Classics

For this chapter, I wanted to reclaim the sweets my kids grew up eating, in our home kitchen, at my former bakery and at other sweet shops in New York City and Italy, where my Dad grew up.

My goal was to streamline each recipe to its purest form to focus on creating the fullest flavor with minimal effort and 100 percent satisfaction. Some of the cookies are so perfect that you won't be able to tell that they are gluten-free. And you definitely will never guess that the super-creamy ice creams in this chapter are dairy-free.

SLICE-AND-BAKE GINGERSNAPS

These gingersnaps are my version of the Nabisco classic—only larger and better. As in the original, there's ginger and molasses, but mine have a bit more spice going on, with the addition of cinnamon, cardamom and cloves. Making logs of cookie dough allows you to slice and bake them as desired so they can always be fresh.

Want more zing? Add 2 teaspoons finely grated peeled fresh ginger or ½ cup finely chopped candied ginger to the dough. If you prefer softer cookies, just bake for a few minutes less. To get a sugary crunch, coat the dough in coarse sugar before baking: Either press the tops of the sliced dough rounds in sugar or roll the log in plenty of sugar before slicing. If you prefer smaller cookies, just divide the dough into 4 equal pieces, then roll into logs about 1 inch in diameter.

Makes: **About twenty-four 2-inch cookies**
Cook Time: **12 minutes**

Prep Time: **16 minutes (plus chilling)**

2 cups My Gluten-Free All-Purpose Flour (page 195)

2 teaspoons baking soda

1 teaspoon salt

2 teaspoons ground ginger

1 teaspoon ground cinnamon

¼ teaspoon ground cardamom

⅛ teaspoon ground cloves

½ cup plus 3 tablespoons shortening, at room temperature

⅔ cup sugar

1 large egg, at room temperature

⅓ cup molasses

1 teaspoon apple cider vinegar

1. In a medium bowl, whisk together the flour, baking soda, salt and spices.

2. In a stand mixer fitted with a paddle attachment, beat together the shortening and sugar, about 3 minutes. Add the egg and beat to combine, scraping down the sides as necessary. On low speed, gradually add the molasses and vinegar. Add the flour mixture on low speed until just combined. Divide the dough into 2 equal pieces and roll into 2 logs about 2 inches in diameter. Wrap in plastic wrap and refrigerate for at least 1 hour. (*The cookie dough logs will keep, tightly wrapped, in the fridge for up to 1 week or frozen in a resealable freezer bag for up to 2 months.*)

3. Preheat the oven to 350°F with racks in the middle and upper third. Line two baking sheets with parchment paper.

4. Cut the dough logs into ½-inch–thick slices and place about 1 inch apart on the baking sheets. Bake, switching the pans from top to bottom and front to back halfway through, until crisp, 10 to 12 minutes. Cool on racks before serving. (*The cookies will keep in an airtight container for up to 1 week.*)

ICED SOFT OATMEAL COOKIES

These cookies have Archway written all over them, thanks to their soft-baked texture and sweet icing, which stays on top without disappearing into the crevices. After some trial and error, I achieved the consistency I wanted by pulsing together the flour, oats and raisins until coarsely ground. If you prefer your cookies crisp, bake for about 2 minutes more.

Makes: **16 cookies**   Prep Time: **12 minutes (plus chilling)**   Cook Time: **14 minutes**

FOR THE COOKIES

- 1 cup My Gluten-Free All-Purpose Flour (page 195)
- ¾ cup gluten-free old-fashioned rolled oats
- 3 tablespoons golden raisins
- ½ cup sugar
- 3 tablespoons shortening
- 2 tablespoons canola oil
- 2 tablespoons brown rice syrup
- 1 teaspoon ground cinnamon
- ¾ teaspoon baking soda
- ½ teaspoon baking powder
- ½ teaspoon salt
- 1 large egg, at room temperature

FOR THE ICING

- 1½ cups confectioners' sugar
- 3 tablespoons water
- 1½ tablespoons shortening, melted

1. **Make the cookies**: Preheat the oven to 350°F with racks in the middle and upper third. Line two baking sheets with parchment paper.

2. Pulse the flour, oats and raisins in a food processor until coarsely ground, about 2 minutes. In a large bowl with an electric mixer, beat together the sugar, shortening, oil, rice syrup, cinnamon, baking soda, baking powder and salt on medium speed until fluffy. Add the egg and mix until blended, about 30 seconds. Reduce the speed to low and mix in the oat mixture until just combined. Refrigerate the dough for 10 minutes.

3. Using a 1½-inch ice cream scoop, drop the dough onto the baking sheets about 2 inches apart. Bake, switching the pans from top to bottom and front to back halfway through, until golden and just set, about 14 minutes. Let cool on the baking sheets for 5 minutes, then transfer to a wire rack set over parchment paper and cool completely.

4. **Meanwhile, make the icing**: Whisk together the confectioners' sugar, water and melted shortening until smooth. Dip the tops of the cookies in the icing to coat, letting the excess drip off. Let set on the rack for at least 30 minutes before serving. (*The cookies will keep in an airtight container layered between sheets of parchment paper for up to 1 week.*)

DEVIL'S FOOD COOKIES

SnackWell's Devil's Food Cookie Cakes were the inspiration for these cookies. The biggest challenge was making the crunchy chocolate shell. The texture of royal icing is similar, so I added some cocoa powder to make it chocolatey, and now it tastes like the real deal.

Makes: **20 cookies**   Prep Time: **30 minutes**   Cook Time: **10 minutes**

FOR THE COOKIES

- 1 cup My Gluten-Free All-Purpose Flour (page 195)
- ⅓ cup unsweetened cocoa powder
- ¾ teaspoon baking soda
- ½ teaspoon salt
- ¼ teaspoon baking powder
- ¾ cup Homemade Cashew or Almond Milk (page 205 or 206) or store-bought, combined with ¾ tablespoon apple cider vinegar
- 1 teaspoon pure vanilla extract
- ½ cup shortening, at room temperature
- 1 cup granulated sugar
- 2 large eggs

FOR THE MARSHMALLOW FILLING

- 6 tablespoons shortening
- ½ cup confectioners' sugar
- ½ teaspoon pure vanilla extract
- ½ cup brown rice syrup
- ½ cup marshmallow creme

FOR THE CHOCOLATE SHELL

- 2 tablespoons powdered egg whites
- 1 cup plus 2 tablespoons warm water
- ½ pound (about 2 cups) confectioners' sugar
- ½ cup unsweetened cocoa powder, sifted

1. **Make the cookies**: Preheat the oven to 350°F with racks in the middle and upper third. Line two baking sheets with parchment paper.

2. In a medium bowl, whisk together the flour, cocoa powder, baking soda, salt and baking powder. In a small bowl, stir together the milk mixture and vanilla.

3. With an electric mixer in a large bowl, mix together the shortening and granulated sugar until fluffy, about 3 minutes. Add the eggs, 1 at a time, beating well after each addition. Mix in one third of the flour mixture, then half of the milk mixture. Repeat with the remaining flour mixture and milk mixture, finishing with the flour mixture.

4. Using a 1½-inch ice cream scoop or tablespoon, drop about 20 generous mounds of batter, spaced evenly, onto the baking sheets. Bake, switching the pans from top to bottom and front to back halfway through, until springy to the touch, about 10 minutes. Transfer to a rack to cool completely.

5.   **Make the marshmallow filling**: With an electric mixer in a medium bowl, beat the shortening on high speed until fluffy, about 3 minutes. On low speed, slowly add the confectioners' sugar until combined, then beat on high speed until fluffy, about 5 minutes. Slowly stream in the vanilla, rice syrup and marshmallow creme. Cover and refrigerate until thickened, about 15 minutes.

6.   Transfer some of the filling to a pastry bag fitted with a ¼-inch plain tip or resealable plastic bag with the corner snipped off, filling the bag less than halfway full. Top each cookie with filling, refilling the bag until all are filled. Refrigerate the cookies until set, about 30 minutes.

7.   **Make the chocolate shell**: With an electric mixer in a large bowl, beat together the powdered egg whites and warm water on medium-low speed until combined and frothy, about 1 minute. Add the confectioners' sugar and beat on medium speed until combined. Add the cocoa powder and beat until combined. Increase the speed to high and beat until thick and glossy, about 5 minutes, for the thick royal icing.

8.   **To assemble**: Line a baking sheet with parchment paper. Submerge the refrigerated cookies in the chocolate shell icing. Remove with a fork, let the excess icing drip off and place on the baking sheet. Let set for about 2 hours. *(The cookies will keep in an airtight container layered between sheets of parchment paper for up to 1 week.)*

VARIATION

Double the recipe. Pour the batter into a greased and floured 8-inch round cake pan. Bake for about 1 hour, or until a toothpick inserted in the center of the cake comes out clean. Let cool completely. Cut the cake horizontally in half and spread the marshmallow filling over the bottom half. Top with the top cake half and pour the chocolate shell over the cake to cover it completely; let set.

DECORATED CUT-OUT SUGAR COOKIES

Cut-out cookies can be as simple or as sophisticated as you want them to be. Just keep in mind the following tips: If the dough softens too much while you're rolling it out, pop it in the fridge for a few minutes to harden. Looking to add more flavor to your cookies? Stir about 1 teaspoon of finely grated lemon or orange zest into the dough. To prevent sticking, dip your cookie cutters into flour before cutting out the cookies. If you're not using the icing right away, cover with plastic wrap, directly on the surface, to prevent a crust from forming.

Makes: **About 2 dozen cookies**   Prep Time: **24 minutes (plus chilling)**   Cook Time: **12 minutes**

2½ cups My Gluten-Free All-Purpose Flour (page 195)

1 1-pound box plus ¾ cup confectioners' sugar

½ cup granulated sugar

¾ teaspoon baking soda

½ teaspoon salt

1 cup shortening

1 large egg

1 teaspoon pure vanilla extract

¼ cup brown rice syrup

¼ cup water

Food coloring (optional)

Decorations, such as sprinkles, sanding sugar (optional)

1. In a bowl, whisk together the flour, ¾ cup of the confectioners' sugar, granulated sugar, baking soda and salt.

2. With an electric mixer in a large bowl, beat the shortening to soften. Beat in the egg and vanilla. Gradually beat in the flour mixture until just combined. Flatten the dough into 2 disks, wrap in plastic wrap and refrigerate for at least 1 hour or overnight.

3. Line two baking sheets with parchment paper.

4. Roll out each piece of dough between two sheets of parchment to about ¼ inch thick. Cut into shapes with cookie cutters and place about 2 inches apart on the baking sheets. Reroll any scraps and cut out more cookies. Refrigerate for 1 hour.

5. Preheat the oven to 350°F with racks in the middle and upper third.

6. Bake the cookies, switching the pans from top to bottom and front to back halfway through, until lightly golden around the edges, 10 to 12 minutes. Let cool on the pans on a wire rack.

7. Meanwhile, in a large bowl with an electric mixer, combine the box of confectioners' sugar, rice syrup and water until smooth. If you like, divide the icing into bowls and tint each one with food coloring. Transfer some of the icing to a pastry bag fitted with a #1 or #2 round tip and outline the border of each cookie; let dry completely. Transfer the remaining icing to a pastry bag fitted with a #4 round tip and flood the outlines with more icing to coat the cookies. Decorate with sprinkles or sanding sugar, if using. Let dry completely, about 3 minutes, before serving. (*The cookies will keep in an airtight container layered between sheets of parchment paper for up to 1 week.*)

BLACK AND WHITE COOKIES

When I was a little girl, my mother always made sure I had my share of these famous cookies that she grew up eating. I keep the tradition going with my kids.

Makes: **10 cookies**   Prep Time: **30 minutes**   Cook Time: **15 minutes**

1 ¼ cups My Gluten-Free All-Purpose Flour (page 195)

½ teaspoon baking soda

½ teaspoon salt

8 tablespoons shortening, at room temperature

¾ cup granulated sugar

1 large egg, at room temperature

1 ½ teaspoons pure vanilla extract

¼ teaspoon pure lemon extract

½ cup store-bought dairy-free creamer combined with 1 ½ tablespoons apple cider vinegar

2 cups confectioners' sugar

2 tablespoons brown rice syrup

2 tablespoons hot water

4 ounces dairy-free semisweet chocolate, chopped

1. Preheat the oven to 350°F with racks in the middle and upper third. Line two baking sheets with parchment paper.

2. In a medium bowl, sift together the flour, baking soda and salt.

3. In a large bowl with an electric mixer, beat 5 tablespoons of the shortening with the granulated sugar on medium-high until fluffy, 3 minutes. Beat in the egg, 1 teaspoon of the vanilla extract and the lemon extract. Beat in the flour mixture alternately with the creamer mixture until smooth.

4. Place ¼-cup scoops of batter 2 inches apart on the baking sheets. Using a small offset spatula or table knife, spread the batter out to form 3-inch circles. Bake, switching the pans from top to bottom and front to back halfway through, until a toothpick inserted in the center of a cookie comes out dry, 12 to 15 minutes. Let the cookies sit for 5 minutes, then transfer to a rack set over parchment paper to cool.

5. In a bowl, whisk together the confectioners' sugar, 1 tablespoon of the rice syrup, the hot water and the remaining ½ teaspoon vanilla until smooth. In another bowl, combine the chocolate, the remaining 3 tablespoons short-ening and the remaining 1 tablespoon rice syrup; microwave until melted, about 1 minute.

6. Using a small offset spatula, coat one half of each cookie with the vanilla icing, then coat the other half with the chocolate icing. Refrigerate until set, about 20 minutes, before serving. *(The cookies will keep in an airtight container layered between sheets of parchment paper for up to 3 days.)*

OLD SCHOOL ITALIAN JAM-FILLED HAZELNUT COOKIES

Each day after school, my son Isaiah and I would go to our local Italian bakery in Carroll Gardens, Brooklyn, to get these cookies. Even with such a big batch, they will disappear before your eyes.

Makes: **About 18 sandwich cookies**   Prep Time: **26 minutes**   Cook Time: **24 minutes**

1½ cups My Gluten-Free All-Purpose Flour (page 195)

1¼ cups finely ground blanched hazelnuts (about 1 cup whole)

1 teaspoon baking powder

½ teaspoon salt

¾ cup shortening, at room temperature

¾ cup confectioners' sugar, sifted

1 large egg, at room temperature

1 teaspoon pure vanilla extract

½ cup seedless raspberry jam, warmed

4 ounces dairy-free semisweet chocolate, melted with 1 tablespoon canola oil or shortening, for dipping

1. Preheat the oven to 325°F with racks in the middle and upper third. Line two baking sheets with parchment paper.

2. Pulse the flour, ground hazelnuts, baking powder and salt in a food processor until blended.

3. In a large bowl with an electric mixer, beat the shortening and sugar on medium-high speed until light and fluffy, about 3 minutes. Reduce the speed to low and beat in the egg and vanilla. Using a wooden spoon, beat in the flour mixture until just combined.

4. Fit a cookie press with the desired disk and fill the press with the dough. Press the dough directly onto the baking sheets, about 2 inches apart. Bake, switching the pans from top to bottom and front to back halfway through, until the cookies are just golden around the edges, about 12 minutes. Transfer to racks and let cool completely. Bake the remaining cookies, letting the baking sheets cool between batches.

5. Sandwich 1 teaspoon warmed jam between 2 cookies. Let set for 15 minutes.

6. Dip the cookies one-third of the way into the melted chocolate mixture, place on a parchment-lined baking sheet and let set at room temperature, about 2 hours, before serving. *(The cookies will keep in an airtight container layered between sheets of parchment paper for up to 1 week.)*

THIN MINTY COOKIES

After spotting kids selling boxes of the Girl Scout Cookies on the streets of Brooklyn, I knew I had to reclaim my childhood memory of snacking on Thin Mints. This recipe yields the perfect mint chocolate cookie, and I show you how to get the shiny coating just right.

Makes: **About sixty 1-inch cookies**   Prep Time: **25 minutes (plus chilling)**
Cook Time: **10 minutes**

1 cup My Gluten-Free All-Purpose Flour (page 195)

½ cup unsweetened cocoa powder

½ teaspoon baking powder

½ teaspoon baking soda

½ teaspoon salt

¾ cup granulated sugar

2½ ounces (5 tablespoons) shortening, at room temperature

1 large egg plus 1 large egg yolk, at room temperature

1 teaspoon pure vanilla extract

¾ teaspoon pure peppermint extract

Confectioners' sugar, for dusting

2 pounds dairy-free semisweet coating chocolate, such as Guittard or Callebaut

1. Preheat the oven to 350°F with racks in the middle and upper third. Line two baking sheets with parchment paper.

2. In a medium bowl, whisk together the flour, cocoa powder, baking powder, baking soda and salt. In a large bowl with an electric mixer, beat together the sugar and shortening on medium speed until fluffy, about 1 minute. Reduce the speed to medium-low and beat in the egg and egg yolk, beating well after each addition. Beat in the vanilla and peppermint extracts. Slowly beat in the flour mixture until just combined. Shape the dough into a disk. Working on a confectioners' sugar–dusted piece of parchment paper, roll out the dough until about ⅛- inch thick. Wrap in plastic wrap and refrigerate until firm, at least 1 hour or overnight.

3. Using a 1½-inch round cutter, cut out cookies and place ½ inch apart on the baking sheets. Reroll any scraps and cut out more cookies. Freeze the cutouts for about 15 minutes. Bake, switching the pans from top to bottom and front to back halfway through, until firm around the edges, 8 to 10 minutes. Let cool slightly; transfer to wire racks to cool completely.

4. Meanwhile, bring water to a low simmer in a double boiler. Place two thirds of the chocolate in the double boiler and melt to 115°F. Stir in the remaining one third of chocolate and let sit for 5 minutes; stir to combine. Let the chocolate cool down to 90°F. Submerge a cookie into the melted chocolate and turn to coat. Shake off any excess and place on parchment paper. Repeat to coat all the cookies, reheating the chocolate to 90°F as needed. Let the cookies set for at least 2 hours. *(The cookies will keep in an airtight container layered between sheets of parchment paper for up to 1 week.)*

PINE NUT COOKIES

These cookies were inspired by an Italian bakery in Rome that my grandfather took me to every Sunday morning before heading to the weekly family brunch. Like the traditional ones, they are crisp outside and meltingly soft within. Swap in 10 ounces of gluten-free store-bought almond paste for the homemade version if you prefer.

Makes: **About 16 cookies**   Prep Time: **14 minutes**   Cook Time: **20 minutes**

FOR THE ALMOND PASTE

1½ cups finely ground blanched almond flour, such as Honeyville

4 ounces (1 cup plus 1 tablespoon) confectioners' sugar

1 large egg white

FOR THE COOKIES

1 cup granulated sugar

¼ teaspoon salt

2 large egg whites

1½ cups pine nuts

Confectioners' sugar, for sprinkling

1. **Make the almond paste**: Pulse the almond flour, confectioners' sugar and egg white in a food processor to combine. (*The almond paste can be made ahead and kept in the fridge, rolled into a log and tightly wrapped in plastic wrap, for up to 3 days.*)

2. **Make the cookies**: Preheat the oven to 325°F with racks in the middle and upper third. Line two baking sheets with parchment paper.

3. Pulse the almond paste, granulated sugar, salt and egg whites in a food processor to combine. Place the pine nuts in a shallow bowl.

4. Using a 1½-inch ice cream scoop or a rounded tablespoon, scoop out portions of the dough and roll in the pine nuts to coat. Place 2 inches apart on the baking sheets and sprinkle with confectioners' sugar. Bake, switching the pans from top to bottom and front to back halfway through, until golden, about 20 minutes. Place the baking sheets on wire racks and let cool completely before serving. (*The cookies will keep in an airtight container for up to 1 week.*)

ROCKY ROAD BROWNIES

As a die-hard brownie fan, I like to expand on classic fudgy brownie texture possibilities and play with different flavor combinations. To finely grind the walnuts, I use my food processor and pulse them together with granulated sugar, which keeps the brownies moist without turning the nuts into oily butter.

Makes: **16 brownies**   Prep Time: **15 minutes**   Cook Time: **50 minutes**

2½   cups chopped walnuts

1¼   cups sugar

¼   cup shortening, melted

1½   cups dairy-free semisweet mini chocolate chips

¼   cup unsweetened cocoa powder

⅓   cup canola oil

3   tablespoons water

½   cup My Gluten-Free All-Purpose Flour (page 195)

¾   teaspoon baking powder

¼   teaspoon salt

3   large eggs, at room temperature

2   teaspoons pure vanilla extract

3   cups mini marshmallows

1. Preheat the oven to 350°F with a rack in the middle. Line an 8-inch square baking pan with a 12-inch-long sheet of parchment paper.

2. Pulse 1½ cups of the walnuts with ¼ cup of the sugar in a food processor until finely ground. Add the melted shortening and pulse until the mixture forms coarse crumbs. Press the crumb mixture into the bottom of the pan. Bake until golden around the edges, about 12 minutes.

3. In a medium microwavable bowl, melt together 1 cup of the chocolate chips, the cocoa powder, oil and water on medium power until almost melted, about 30 seconds. Whisk until smooth. Let cool to room temperature, about 3 minutes.

4. In a small bowl, whisk together the remaining 1 cup sugar, the flour, baking powder and salt.

5. Whisk the eggs and vanilla into the cooled chocolate mixture. Add the flour mixture, remaining ½ cup chocolate chips and remaining 1 cup walnuts; stir to combine. Spread the batter evenly over the crumb bottom. Bake until set, about 35 minutes, or until a toothpick comes out with wet crumbs.

6. Preheat the broiler.

7. Top the brownies with the marshmallows and broil until toasted, about 2 minutes. Let cool on a wire rack for about 15 minutes. Use the parchment to carefully remove the brownies and then cut into 16 squares.

VARIATION

S'MORES BROWNIES: Instead of the nut mixture, line the prepared brownie pan with a layer of gluten-free homemade or store-bought graham crackers. Top with the brownie batter. Bake until set, about 35 minutes, top with mini marshmallows and bake for 10 minutes more, or until the marshmallows are melty and golden.

Brownie Bark (page 172)

BROWNIE BARK

I was fascinated when I first spotted Sheila G's Chocolate Chip Brownie Brittle at the super-market. A brownie that doubles as a crisp cookie? I love that idea! To replicate it, I replaced the whole eggs in my classic brownie recipe with egg whites and spread the brownie batter thin to get a nice crunch.

Serves: 8   Prep Time: **7 minutes**   Cook Time: **25 minutes**

½ cup dairy-free semisweet mini chocolate chips, plus more for sprinkling

2 tablespoons unsweetened cocoa powder

2½ tablespoons canola oil

1½ teaspoons water

2 large egg whites, at room temperature, beaten until frothy

½ cup sugar

6 tablespoons My Gluten-Free All-Purpose Flour (page 195)

⅛ teaspoon baking soda

¼ teaspoon salt

1. Preheat the oven to 300°F with racks in the middle and upper third. Line two baking sheets with parchment paper.

2. In a medium microwavable bowl, melt together the chocolate chips, cocoa powder, oil and water on medium power until almost melted, about 30 seconds; whisk until smooth and let cool.

3. Whisk the egg whites, sugar, flour, baking soda and salt into the melted chocolate until smooth and shiny. Spread the batter evenly on the baking sheets and sprinkle with some chocolate chips. Bake, switching the pans from top to bottom and front to back halfway through, until crisp around the edges, about 25 minutes. Cool completely on a rack. To serve, break apart into pieces. *(The bark will keep in an airtight container for up to 1 week.)*

CHOCOLATE-COCONUT-OAT MAGIC BARS

Traditional magic bars—those impossibly rich, no-brainer-to-make sweets composed of layered chocolate chips, coconut and graham crackers—were off-limits until I figured out how to make Dairy-Free Condensed Milk.

Makes: **16 bars** Prep Time: **8 minutes** Cook Time: **30 minutes**

1 cup finely ground gluten-free graham cracker crumbs

½ cup gluten-free quick-cooking oats

⅛ teaspoon salt

⅓ cup shortening, melted

1 cup dairy-free semisweet chocolate chips

1 cup sweetened flaked coconut

½ cup chopped blanched hazelnuts, toasted (optional)

1 cup Dairy-Free Condensed Milk (page 207) or store-bought

1. Preheat the oven to 350°F with a rack in the middle. Line an 8-inch square baking pan with a 12-inch-long sheet of parchment paper.

2. In a small bowl, combine the cracker crumbs, oats, salt and melted shortening. Press into the pan. Scatter the chocolate chips, coconut and hazelnuts, if using, over the mixture. Pour the condensed milk evenly over the top.

3. Bake until golden, 25 to 30 minutes. Let cool for about 15 minutes before cutting into 16 squares and serving.

GOLDEN VANILLA BIRTHDAY CAKE WITH VANILLA FROSTING

Everyone needs a basic, all-purpose vanilla cake. To get a wonderfully cakey, moist texture, I use a combination of shortening and vegetable oil. Sometimes I add scraped vanilla bean seeds to give the cake a flecked vanilla look. Want to go beyond vanilla? Flavor your frosting with about 1 teaspoon of your favorite extract, such as mint, almond or orange.

Makes: One 8-inch 4-layer cake   **Prep Time: 24 minutes**   **Cook Time: 38 minutes**

FOR THE CAKE

- 3 cups My Gluten-Free All-Purpose Flour (page 195)
- 2 cups sugar
- 1 tablespoon baking powder
- 1 teaspoon salt
- ½ cup shortening
- ½ cup canola oil
- 4 large eggs, at room temperature
- 1 tablespoon pure vanilla extract
- ¾ cup cup Homemade Cashew or Almond Milk (page 205 or 206) or store-bought

FOR THE FROSTING

- ½ cup My Gluten-Free All-Purpose Flour (page 195)
- 2 cups sugar
- 2 cup cup Homemade Cashew or Almond Milk (page 205 or 206) or store-bought
- 2 cups shortening
- 1 tablespoon pure vanilla extract
- Cake toppers, such as sprinkles, edible glitter, crushed gluten-free cookie crumbs, berries or chopped nuts

1. **Make the cakes:** Preheat the oven to 350°F with a rack in the middle. Spray two 8-inch round cake pans with cooking spray.
2. In a large bowl, whisk together the flour, sugar, baking powder and salt. Add the shortening and oil and beat with an electric mixer until light and fluffy. Add the eggs, 1 at a time, beating well after each addition, then beat in the vanilla. Add the milk, mixing until just combined.
3. Divide the batter between the two pans, smoothing the tops. Bake until the cakes are springy to the touch and a toothpick inserted

in the center comes out clean, 32 to 38 minutes. Cool the cakes in the pans on racks for about 10 minutes. Invert onto the rack, invert again and cool completely.

4. **Meanwhile, make the frosting**: In a small saucepan, whisk the flour and sugar together. Stir in the milk and cook over medium heat, stirring, until hot and thickened, about 8 minutes. Transfer to a large bowl and beat on high speed with the mixer until cooled. Gradually add the shortening and vanilla on low speed until incorporated, about 3 minutes. Beat on medium-high speed until light and fluffy, about 3 minutes.

5. **Assemble the cake**: Trim the tops of the cooled cake layers with a long serrated knife to make them flat and level if necessary. Halve each layer horizontally with the knife to make a total of 4 layers. Put 1 cake layer on a cake plate and spread ³/₄ cup frosting on top. Layer the remaining cake layers, spreading ³/₄ cup frosting between each layer. Frost the top and sides of cake with the remaining frosting. Scatter some cake toppers over the cake and serve.

SPICE LAYER CAKE WITH PECAN PRALINE AND MARSHMALLOW FROSTING

There are three parts to this cake, but it's worth every second in the kitchen. Add it to your dessert repertoire for the holiday season. If you're wondering whether you can omit the orange zest, don't do it. It brightens all of the spiciness going on here. Feeling fancy? If you have a kitchen torch, go ahead and toast the marshmallow frosting until golden.

Makes: One 8-inch 3-layer cake · **Prep Time: 50 minutes** · **Cook Time: 30 minutes**

FOR THE PRALINE

- 1 cup granulated sugar
- 1 cup pecan halves (about 8 ounces)

FOR THE CAKE

- 2½ cups My Gluten-Free All-Purpose Flour (page 195)
- 1 tablespoon pumpkin pie spice
- 2 teaspoons baking powder
- 1 teaspoon baking soda
- 1 teaspoon salt
- 1 cup shortening, at room temperature
- 1 cup granulated sugar
- ½ cup packed light brown sugar
- Grated zest of 1 orange
- 4 large eggs, at room temperature
- ¾ cup plus 2 tablespoons Homemade Cashew or Almond Milk (page 205 or 206) or store-bought
- 1 15-ounce can pure pumpkin puree

FOR THE FROSTING

- 4 large egg whites, at room temperature
- 1 cup granulated sugar
- Pinch of cream of tartar

1. **Make the praline:** Line a baking sheet with parchment paper. In a large skillet, melt the granulated sugar over medium-high heat until light amber, about 7 minutes. Reduce the heat to low, add the pecans and quickly stir to coat. Transfer the pecans to the baking sheet and, using a metal spatula, spread in a single layer; cool completely. Place the praline in a sturdy resealable plastic bag and crush into pieces.

2. **Make the cake:** Preheat the oven to 350°F with racks in the middle and upper third. Spray three 8-inch round cake pans with cooking spray. Line the bottoms of the pans with parchment paper and spray the parchment with cooking spray. Flour the pans.

3. In a bowl, sift together the flour, pumpkin pie spice, baking powder, baking soda and salt. In a large bowl with an electric mixer on medium-high speed, beat together the shortening,

continued

granulated sugar, brown sugar and orange zest until light and fluffy, about 3 minutes. Add the eggs, 1 at a time, beating until combined. On low speed, beat in the flour mixture in 3 parts, alternating with the milk until combined. Add the pumpkin puree and beat until just combined.

4. Divide the batter evenly among the three pans. Bake, switching the pans from top to bottom and front to back halfway through, until a toothpick inserted in the center comes out clean, about 30 minutes. Transfer the cake layers to a rack to cool for about 10 minutes. Remove the cakes from the pans, invert and peel off the parchment paper. Invert again and let the cakes cool completely on the rack, about 45 minutes.

5. **Meanwhile, make the frosting**: Combine the egg whites, granulated sugar and cream of tartar in a large heatproof bowl set over a saucepan of simmering water. Whisk continuously until the sugar has dissolved, about 3 minutes. Remove from the heat and, with the mixer on high speed, beat until stiff peaks form, about 6 minutes.

6. **Assemble the cake**: Trim the tops of the cooled cake layers with a long serrated knife to make them flat and level if necessary. Place 1 cake layer on a serving platter. Evenly spread one third of the frosting on top. Sprinkle with about ½ cup crushed pecan praline. Repeat with the remaining cake layers and serve.

BROWN SUGAR POUND CAKE WITH CRANBERRIES AND PISTACHIO CRUNCH

Holiday flavors give this cake a festive character. The nutty crunchy topping is modeled after the one on a traditional Italian Easter cake—ground almonds, sugar and egg whites—but instead of almonds, I use pistachios which add a beautiful muted green color and sweet flavor.

Makes: **One 9-by-5-inch loaf**   Prep Time: **10 minutes**   Cook Time: **55 minutes**

1½ cups My Gluten-Free All-Purpose Flour (page 195)

 1 tablespoon ground cinnamon

 2 teaspoons baking powder

½ teaspoon salt

 4 large eggs plus 1 egg white, at room temperature

 1 cup packed light brown sugar

½ cup canola oil

 1 tablespoon pure vanilla extract

½ cup fresh or frozen cranberries

½ cup shelled pistachios

¼ cup granulated sugar

1. Preheat the oven to 350°F with rack in the middle. Spray a 9-by-5-inch loaf pan with cooking spray.
2. In a small bowl, whisk together the flour, cinnamon, baking powder and salt.
3. In a large bowl, whisk together the 4 eggs and the brown sugar until frothy. Slowly whisk in the oil and vanilla. Whisk the flour mixture into the egg mixture until just combined. Stir in the cranberries. Scrape the batter into the loaf pan.
4. Chop ¼ cup of the pistachios. With a food processor, finely grind the chopped pistachios with the granulated sugar. Add the egg white and process until smooth. Drizzle over the top of the cake and sprinkle with the remaining ¼ cup chopped pistachios.
5. Bake until a toothpick inserted in the center comes out clean, about 55 minutes. Let cool completely on a rack. Run a knife around the sides of the pan and transfer to a serving plate.

PUMPKIN PIE CANNOLI WITH MAPLE-CANDIED PISTACHIOS

I grew up eating classically flavored cannoli from the Italian bakeries in Rome and Brooklyn, especially as a festive dessert around Christmas. I wanted to make some for Thanksgiving one holiday season, so I gave them an American twist with the flavors of pumpkin pie. The Dairy-Free Sweet Ricotta Cheese—with its orange zest and vanilla—was developed with this recipe in mind.

Serves: **4 to 6 (24 cannoli)**   Prep Time: **24 minutes (plus resting)**   Cook Time: **15 minutes**

FOR THE FILLING

- 1 recipe Dairy-Free Sweet Ricotta Cheese (page 216), drained
- ¼ cup canned pure pumpkin puree, drained
- 1 cup confectioners' sugar, sifted, plus more for dusting
- 1 teaspoon pure vanilla extract
- ½ teaspoon pumpkin pie spice
- 3 tablespoons chopped dairy-free semisweet chocolate

FOR THE MAPLE-CANDIED PISTACHIOS

- ½ cup salted shelled pistachios
- 2 teaspoons pure maple syrup

FOR THE SHELLS

- 2 cups My Gluten-Free All-Purpose Flour (page 195)
- 2 tablespoons granulated sugar
- ½ teaspoon pumpkin pie spice
- 2 tablespoons cold shortening, cut into ½-inch pieces
- 2 large egg yolks plus 1 whole egg beaten with 1 teaspoon water, for egg wash
- ½ cup plus 1 tablespoon Marsala or white wine

  Canola oil, for frying

1. **Make the filling**: In a medium bowl, stir together the ricotta cheese, pumpkin puree, confectioners' sugar, vanilla and pumpkin pie spice until smooth. Stir in the chocolate. Cover and refrigerate.

2. **Make the maple-candied pistachios**: Preheat the oven to 400°F with a rack in the middle. Lightly spray a baking sheet with cooking spray.

3. In a small bowl, toss together the pistachios and maple syrup to coat. Spread evenly on the baking sheet. Toast in the oven until shiny, about 3 minutes. Let cool completely. Coarsely chop.

Pumpkin Pie Cannoli with Maple-Candied
Pistachios (page 181)

4. **Meanwhile, make the shells:** Sift the flour, granulated sugar and pumpkin pie spice into a large bowl. Add the shortening pieces and, using a fork, combine until coarse crumbs form. In a small bowl, beat together the 2 egg yolks and Marsala; gradually incorporate into the flour mixture until a dough forms. Cover with plastic wrap and let rest for about 30 minutes.

5. Roll out the dough until about $\frac{1}{8}$ inch thick and, using a glass or bowl, cut into about twenty-four 4-inch rounds. Roll the dough around greased $\frac{3}{4}$-inch cannoli tubes or dried gluten-free manicotti pasta shells. Seal with a little of the beaten egg wash.

6. Heat 3 inches of oil in a deep, heavy-bottomed pan to 350°F. Working with 4 at a time, add the shells to the hot oil and fry, turning, until golden brown, about $1\frac{1}{2}$ minutes. Remove with a slotted spoon or tongs and let cool slightly. Carefully slide the shells off the tubes and drain on paper towels. Let cool completely.

7. Just before serving, pipe the filling into each shell. Dip the ends in the candied pistachios, dust with confectioners' sugar and serve.

CHERRY PIE POPPERS

A brown sugar shortbread crust sends these sweet mouthfuls over the edge. The pastry dough has a crumbly cookie-like texture. Instead of frozen, you can use fresh, in-season cherries or even swap in your favorite fruit.

Makes: **24 pie poppers**   Prep Time: **18 minutes**   Cook Time: **32 minutes**

FOR THE FILLING

- 1   12-ounce bag (about 2 cups) frozen pitted cherries, thawed, drained and chopped
- ⅓   cup granulated sugar
- ⅛   teaspoon pumpkin pie spice
- 2   teaspoons lemon juice
- 1   teaspoon pure vanilla extract
- 1   tablespoon cornstarch blended with 2 teaspoons water

FOR THE CRUST

- 1   cup shortening, softened
- 1   cup packed light brown sugar
- 1   teaspoon pure vanilla extract
- 2   cups My Gluten-Free All-Purpose Flour (page 195)
- ⅓   cup cornstarch
- ¼   teaspoon salt

1. **Make the filling**: In a medium saucepan, stir together the cherries, granulated sugar, pumpkin pie spice, lemon juice and vanilla. Cook over medium heat, stirring, until the sugar is dissolved, about 5 minutes. Stir in the cornstarch mixture and cook until thickened and the cherries have softened, about 4 minutes. Let cool.

2. **Make the crust**: Preheat the oven to 350°F with a rack in the middle. Spray a 24-cup mini muffin pan with cooking spray.

3. In a large bowl with an electric mixer on medium speed, beat together the shortening, brown sugar and vanilla until light and fluffy, about 3 minutes. On low speed, mix in the flour, cornstarch and salt until the dough is shaggy.

4. Press a heaping 1 tablespoon of the dough into the bottoms and up the sides of each muffin cup. Bake until set, about 8 minutes. Let cool slightly.

5. Add about 2 teaspoons filling to each crust. Bake for 15 minutes, or until bubbling and golden. Let cool for 15 minutes, then run a knife around each muffin cup to remove from the pan and serve.

APPLE BEIGNETS

Instead of using my all-purpose flour to coat the apples before frying, I prefer to use my pancake and waffle mix. The bits of shortening add pockets of fat that melt just as the beignets hit the hot oil, making them extra crunchy.

Serves: **4** • Prep Time: **12 minutes** • Cook Time: **26 minutes**

1 cup My Gluten-Free Pancake, Waffle and Biscuit Mix (page 196)

½ cup plus 2 tablespoons Homemade Cashew or Almond Milk (page 205 or 206) or store-bought

1 large egg, at room temperature

1 tablespoon pure vanilla extract

Vegetable oil, for frying

½ cup granulated sugar

1 tablespoon ground cinnamon

3 apples, peeled, cored and cut into ¼-inch-thick rings

Confectioners' sugar, for dusting

1. Place the pancake mix in a medium bowl. In a small bowl, whisk together the milk, egg and vanilla. Add the milk mixture to the pancake mix and beat well.

2. Heat 2 inches of oil in a deep frying pan to 360°F, or until a drop of batter immediately rises to the surface.

3. In a large bowl, whisk together the sugar and cinnamon. Toss the apple rings with the cinnamon sugar to coat. In batches, dip the apple rings into the batter and gently place into the hot oil. Fry, turning once, until golden, about 2 minutes on each side. Drain on paper towels. Keep warm in a 200°F oven while you fry the remaining rings.

4. Dust with confectioners' sugar and serve.

VARIATION

BANANA BEIGNETS: Swap bananas, sliced on the diagonal, for the apple rings.

KEY LIME PIE CREAMSICLES

This recipe was never intended to be: It just happened. I had made a dairy-free lemon cream filling for a cake, had some left over and decided to freeze it. Isaiah came home from school and tried it. One lick, and he announced, "Tastes like key lime pie!" All I had to do then was substitute lime juice for the lemon juice and there it was, key lime pie in creamsicle form.

To add some crust, finely crush store-bought or homemade (page 153) gluten-free ginger-snap cookies and sprinkle the crumbs between the layers of custard in the mold.

Makes: **6 creamsicles**   Prep Time: **5 minutes (plus freezing)**   Cook Time: **10 minutes**

3 large eggs plus 1 large egg yolk

1 cup sugar

1 tablespoon lime zest

½ cup freshly squeezed lime juice (about 6 limes)

1. Place a large heatproof bowl over a pot of simmering water. Add the 3 eggs and the egg yolk, the sugar, lime zest and juice. Whisking constantly, cook until thickened, about 10 minutes. Remove from the heat and let cool slightly.

2. Transfer to a container, cover the surface directly with plastic wrap and refrigerate until chilled, about 1 hour. Divide among six ice-pop molds and freeze until solid, about 4 hours or overnight.

VERY VANILLA CHOCOLATE CHIP ICE CREAM

After taste-testing dairy-free ice creams from supermarkets and health food stores that were made from hemp milk, coconut milk, almond milk, rice milk and cashew milk, I found them all to be a bit icier and much less creamy than I liked. I loved the rich, high-fat homemade cashew milk I had been making and decided to try it in ice cream. Several batches later, I realized that the quantity of sugar and egg yolks also had a major impact on texture, so I increased them until the mixture coated the spoon. As with all homemade ice creams, this one is best enjoyed if you let it sit on your kitchen countertop for 5 to 10 minutes before serving—or pop it in the microwave on high for about 10 seconds.

Makes: **About 1 pint**   Prep Time: **45 minutes (plus chilling and freezing)**   Cook Time: **10 minutes**

2   cups Homemade Cashew Milk
     (page 205)

     Seeds of 1 vanilla bean

     Pinch of salt

¾   cup sugar

5   large egg yolks

1½   teaspoons pure vanilla extract

3½   ounces dairy-free semisweet
     chocolate, chopped and melted

1. In a heavy medium saucepan, combine the milk, vanilla bean seeds and salt. Bring to a simmer.

2. In a medium bowl, whisk together the sugar and egg yolks until thick and pale. Gradually whisk in the heated milk mixture in a slow, steady stream. Pour the mixture back into the saucepan. Cook over low heat, whisking, until the custard is thickened and coats the back of a spoon, 6 to 8 minutes. Let cool slightly, then transfer to a container and cover the surface directly with plastic wrap. Refrigerate until cold, at least 2 hours.

3. Strain the custard mixture through a fine-mesh strainer, pressing with a rubber spatula. Pour the custard into an ice cream machine with the vanilla extract. Process until it has the texture of soft-serve ice cream, 20 to 25 minutes. Transfer the ice cream to an airtight container, drizzling in the melted chocolate between the layers and breaking it up as it hardens. Freeze until firm, at least 4 hours, before serving.

VARIATION

MINT CHOCOLATE CHIP ICE CREAM: Stir ½ cup chopped fresh mint leaves into the milk in Step 1, cover and let steep for 30 minutes. Strain out the mint, then rewarm the milk before whisking into the egg–sugar mixture.

CHOCOLATE–PEANUT BUTTER ICE CREAM

This is a Reese's peanut butter cup in ice cream form. The double hit from the cocoa powder and semisweet chocolate makes it super chocolatey. Drizzling in the peanut butter mixture ensures creamy peanut butter in every bite.

Makes: About 1 pint   Prep Time: **45 minutes (plus chilling and freezing)**   Cook Time: **10 minutes**

2 cups Homemade Cashew Milk (page 205)

⅓ cup unsweetened cocoa powder

2 ounces dairy-free semisweet chocolate, chopped

Pinch of salt

¾ cup granulated sugar

5 large egg yolks

½ cup creamy peanut butter

2 tablespoons confectioners' sugar

1. In a heavy medium saucepan, combine the milk, cocoa powder, chocolate and salt; bring to a simmer.

2. In a medium bowl, whisk together the granulated sugar and egg yolks until thick and pale. Gradually whisk in the heated milk mixture in a slow, steady stream. Pour the mixture back into the saucepan. Cook over low heat, whisking, until the custard is thickened and coats the back of a spoon, 6 to 8 minutes. Let cool slightly, then transfer to a container and cover the surface directly with plastic wrap. Refrigerate until cold, at least 2 hours.

3. Strain the custard mixture through a fine-mesh strainer, pressing with a rubber spatula. Pour into an ice cream machine and process until it has the texture of soft-serve ice cream, 20 to 25 minutes.

4. Meanwhile, in a small saucepan, melt together the peanut butter and confectioners' sugar, stirring until smooth.

5. Transfer the ice cream to an airtight container, drizzling in the peanut butter mixture between layers. Freeze until firm, at least 4 hours, before serving.

CHOCOLATE CHIP–COOKIE DOUGH ICE CREAM SANDWICHES

I use blanched almond flour for the cookie dough instead of all-purpose flour because the resulting texture is extremely pliable, which is just what you want when you're biting into a cookie ice cream sandwich.

Makes: **8 ice cream sandwiches**   Prep Time: **12 minutes (plus freezing)**   Cook Time: **8 minutes**

3 cups blanched almond flour, preferably Honeyville

1½ teaspoons baking powder

¾ teaspoon baking soda

¾ teaspoon salt

6 tablespoons shortening

3 tablespoons honey

1½ teaspoons pure vanilla extract

1½ teaspoons light molasses

1 cup coarsely chopped dairy-free semisweet chocolate

Dairy-free mini chocolate chips, for decorating

1 pint dairy-free vanilla ice cream, softened

1. Preheat the oven to 350°F with racks in the middle and upper third. Line two baking sheets with parchment paper.

2. Pulse the almond flour, baking powder, baking soda and salt in a food processor to blend. Add the shortening, honey, vanilla and molasses and pulse until a dough forms. Transfer to a large bowl and, using a wooden spoon, stir in the chopped chocolate.

3. Break one third of the cookie dough into chunks and stir into the ice cream. Freeze until firm, about 4 hours.

4. Meanwhile, using a 1½-inch scoop or a rounded tablespoon, drop the remaining cookie dough 2 inches apart onto the baking sheets. Press down on the dough gently to flatten slightly. Bake until golden around the edges, about 8 minutes. Let cool for about 10 minutes. Using a spatula, transfer to a wire rack to cool.

5. Place the mini chocolate chips in a shallow bowl. Scoop about ¼ cup of the ice cream onto a cookie, flat side up, then sandwich with another cookie. Roll the sides in the chocolate chips to coat. Repeat with the remaining cookies and ice cream. Freeze on a baking sheet for at least 30 minutes before serving. (*The ice cream sandwiches can be frozen in a resealable freezer bag for up to 2 weeks.*)

Reinvented Baking Mixes

MY GLUTEN-
FREE ALL-PURPOSE
FLOUR

MY GLUTEN-FREE
EL & PRETZEL
MIX

MY GLUTEN FREE
SEASONED FLOUR

BACK TO BASICS

I've always loved the basic ingredients and easy baking steps that result from using a mix. Over the years, I've developed my cheat-sheet versions of the store-bought favorites I grew up on. I've listed both weights and volumes in the recipes, because when you're making a large quantity, measuring by weight speeds things up. For all of my mixes, though, I've developed a built-in margin of error, so if you decide to measure by volume, the mix will work equally well.

GLUTEN-FREE BAKING AND COOKING MIXES

MY GLUTEN-FREE ALL-PURPOSE FLOUR

It took me months of trial and error to develop this flour blend. Since then, I've tested a bunch of store-bought flour mixes, and mine still outperforms them in terms of flavor and texture. Now I'm going to get technical for a minute. When making your own, in my experience, the classic ratio that mimics regular unbleached all-purpose flour is 60 percent grain flour (white rice, brown rice) and 40 percent starch (tapioca flour, potato starch). If you decide to use a gum, which I recommend, since it helps with overall texture, add about ½ teaspoon of xanthan or guar gum per 1 cup flour blend. My flour blend is an old-school mix of white starches, but if you want to add more fiber, replace the 6 cups of white rice flour with half white rice flour and half brown rice flour.

Makes: **About 10 cups**   Prep Time: **12 minutes**

6 cups (870 g) white rice flour

3 cups (375 g) tapioca flour

1½ cups (246 g) potato starch

1 tablespoon (9 g) salt

2 tablespoons (18 g) xanthan gum

In a large bowl, whisk together all the ingredients. Transfer to an airtight storage container. (*The flour keeps in a cool, dry place or refrigerated for up to 6 months.*)

MY GLUTEN-FREE PANCAKE, WAFFLE AND BISCUIT MIX

I've always been a fan of Bisquick, but after trying the gluten-free version from the supermarket, I wasn't convinced it was a perfect substitute. So I studied the ingredients on the original and replicated its taste and texture. One bite of a pancake made me want to open a chain of gluten-free IHOPs (International House of Pancakes). Perfect pancakes (page 11), crisp waffles (page 27) and fluffy biscuits (page 29) followed.

Makes: **About 16 cups**   Prep Time: **8 minutes**

10 cups (1572 g) My Gluten-Free All-Purpose Flour (page 195)

1 cup (212 g) sugar

6 tablespoons (72 g) baking powder

4 teaspoons (12 g) salt

1 cup (172 g) shortening

In a food processor, mix the flour, sugar, baking powder and salt. Add the shortening and pulse until uniform in texture. Transfer to an airtight storage container. (*The mix keeps in a cool, dry place or refrigerated for up to 6 months.*)

MY GLUTEN-FREE SANDWICH LOAF BREAD AND PIZZA MIX

Developing a sandwich bread recipe was becoming my full-time job, which inevitably included tossing dozens of unsatisfactory loaves in the garbage. Then one morning I decided to throw all of my tricks into one recipe—and it worked. Yes, the ingredient list is long, but you won't regret making this mix the second you slice into the just-baked bread. So what are my secrets? To make a high-protein bread flour, which helps with overall texture, I added rice protein powder. The vitamin C and baking powder give the bread a nice boost in height when the bread is baking, and the flaxseed meal and psyllium husk powder add body and contribute structure.

Makes: **About 3½ cups**   Prep Time: **10 minutes**

1 cup plus 2 tablespoons (160 g) cornstarch

½ cup (90 g) potato starch

½ cup (80 g) rice flour

½ cup (70 g) millet flour

¼ cup (53 g) golden flaxseed meal

¼ cup (27 g) raw organic rice protein powder, such as Growing Naturals

2 tablespoons (18 g) psyllium husk powder

2 teaspoons (10 g) baking powder

1½ teaspoons (9 g) salt

1 teaspoon (3 g) xanthan gum

2 tablespoons (30 g) granulated sugar

1 ¼-ounce (8.75 g) package active dry yeast

¼ teaspoon (500 mg) vitamin C powder

In a large bowl, whisk together all the ingredients. Transfer to an airtight storage container. *(The mix keeps in a cool, dry place or refrigerated for up to 6 months.)*

MY GLUTEN-FREE BAGEL AND PRETZEL MIX

Because the texture of bagels and pretzels differs from sandwich bread, I have developed a unique flour blend for them. Much as with yogurt, the probiotics powder adds a slight tang and a nice lift to the rising dough. The psyllium husk powder absorbs moisture, while simultaneously swelling the dough, letting you roll and shape it with your hands, a rare occasion in gluten-free bread baking.

Makes: **About 3¾ cups**   Prep Time: **15 minutes**

1½ cups (210 g) cornstarch

¾ cup (120 g) potato starch

¾ cup (105 g) white rice flour

½ cup (70 g) millet flour or sorghum flour

2 tablespoons (18 g) psyllium husk powder

2½ teaspoons (10 g) salt

1½ teaspoons sugar

1 ¼-ounce (8.75 g) packet active dry yeast

1 teaspoon (3 g) xanthan gum (optional)

1 teaspoon (3 g) dairy-free probiotics powder (optional)

In a large bowl, whisk together all the ingredients. Transfer to an airtight storage container. *(The mix keeps in a cool, dry place or refrigerated for up to 6 months.)*

MY GLUTEN-FREE SEASONED FLOUR

I wanted a super-convenient, versatile flour to use for coating, like Shake 'n Bake, that I could easily grab from the pantry. I studied the ingredient list on the packaging and batch by batch worked to replicate the flavor. Go ahead and substitute your favorite spices, but don't omit the sugar, since it rounds out all the flavors.

Makes: **About 4 cups**   Prep Time: **8 minutes**

2 cups My Gluten-Free All-Purpose Flour (page 195)

1 cup corn flour or more gluten-free all-purpose flour

¼ cup paprika

1 tablespoon celery salt

1 tablespoon mustard powder

1 tablespoon baking powder

1 tablespoon salt

1 teaspoon black pepper

1 teaspoon garlic powder

1 teaspoon crushed dried thyme leaves

1 teaspoon confectioners' sugar

1½ teaspoons cayenne (optional)

In a large bowl, whisk together all the ingredients. Transfer to an airtight storage container. *(The flour keeps in a cool, dry place or refrigerated for up to 6 months.)*

MY GLUTEN-FREE BREAD CRUMBS

I like to keep these flavored bread crumbs in my pantry at all times to make cooking dinner a cinch. I've purposely kept the ingredients simple so that the flavors don't overpower whatever main ingredient you're coating. For a change, replace the paprika with smoked paprika.

Makes: **About 3 cups** · Prep Time: **5 minutes** · Cook Time: **25 minutes**

1 loaf Sandwich Loaf Bread (page 40) or store-bought gluten-free bread, sliced, crusts trimmed

1 tablespoon paprika

1 tablespoon salt

1 teaspoon black pepper

1 teaspoon confectioners' sugar

1. Preheat the oven to 350°F.
2. Place the bread slices in a single layer on a baking sheet and toast in the oven, turning once, until crisp, about 20 minutes. Let cool completely on a wire rack.
3. Working in batches, if necessary, place the toasts in a food processor. Add the paprika, salt, pepper and confectioners' sugar and process until small crumbs form. Transfer to an airtight storage container. (*The bread crumbs keep in a cool, dry place or refrigerated for up to 6 months.*)

DAIRY-FREE BASICS

I've tried a number of dairy-free substitutes in the market, and many seem to lack the richness of the real foods. I turned to cultures around the world and studied fermented foods, evenutally developing my own formulations of dairy-free milk, cheese, yogurt and more.

For many of the following recipes, a high-speed blender such as a Vitamix is essential to properly emulsify the nut milks so they become super-creamy.

DAIRY-FREE MILK, CHEESE, YOGURT AND MORE

HOMEMADE CASHEW MILK

There's always a bottle of cashew milk in my fridge. It's the most versatile nut milk, the fastest to prepare and the easiest to clean up. Because of their high-fat content, cashews are creamy in texture, which makes them perfect for making dairy-free ice cream, condensed milk and dulce de leche. Sometimes I spice things up by stirring in some cinnamon. If I'm in a rush, I use a heaping ¼ cup of cashew butter instead of raw cashews.

Makes: **4 cups**   Prep Time: **5 minutes (plus soaking)**

1 cup raw cashews, soaked for at least 4 hours or overnight, rinsed and drained

4 cups water

2–3 tablespoons agave nectar (optional)

Seeds of 1 vanilla bean or 2 teaspoons pure vanilla extract

¼ teaspoon salt

Add all the ingredients to a high-speed blender and process on high speed until smooth, about 1 minute. Pour through a sieve. *(The milk keeps, refrigerated, in a resealable container for up to 1 week.)*

YOUR NUT MILK GUIDE	
For	*Follow the recipe above, using*
nonfat milk	5 cups water
low-fat milk	4 cups water
whole milk	3 cups water
heavy cream	2–2½ cups water

HOMEMADE ALMOND MILK

This was the first dairy-free milk I ever created. I love the flavor—and that it's high in protein. Making it from scratch, which involves separating the freshly blended milk from the raw almond skins, can get a little messy. That said, it's well worth the effort.

You can substitute pistachios, hazelnuts or Brazil nuts for the almonds. If you don't have a nut bag, use a jelly strainer bag or multiple layers of cheesecloth to strain until smooth. Besides the possibilities below, you can also flavor the milk, if you like, by stirring in ¼ teaspoon pure vanilla or almond extract, or 2 tablespoons maple syrup or honey in place of the agave.

Makes: About 4 cups   **Prep Time: 5 minutes (plus soaking)**

1 cup raw almonds, soaked for at least 4 hours or overnight, rinsed and drained

4 cups water

2 tablespoons agave nectar (optional)

¼ teaspoon salt

1. Place the almonds and water in a high-speed blender; process until smooth, about 2 minutes.
2. Using a nut milk bag or cheesecloth set in a strainer, strain. Rinse the blender, then return the almond milk to the blender, add the agave nectar, if using, and the salt, and blend to combine. *(The milk keeps refrigerated in a resealable container for up to 1 week. If it separates, shake to combine.)*

DIY FLAVORED MILKS

CHOCOLATE MILK Add 1 tablespoon cocoa power to 1 cup strained milk; blend to combine.

STRAWBERRY MILK Add ½ cup hulled fresh or frozen strawberries to 1 cup strained milk; blend to combine.

DAIRY-FREE BUTTERMILK

Just as buttermilk gives any recipe a lift—literally, the acid from the vinegar here boosts any baked good and lends a nice tanginess. This version does not have buttermilk's viscosity, unless you add a thickener, which I prefer to leave out. If you want it, blend in xanthan gum, a pinch at a time, until you reach the desired consistency. You can use lemon juice or distilled white vinegar in place of the apple cider vinegar.

Makes: **About 2 cups**   Prep Time: **2 minutes**

2 cups Homemade Cashew or Almond Milk (page 205 or 206) or store-bought, preferably whole-milk or heavy-cream consistency

2 tablespoons apple cider vinegar

In a small bowl, whisk together the milk and vinegar. Let stand until the mixture begins to slightly curdle, about 10 minutes. Use immediately or refrigerate. *(The buttermilk will keep refrigerated in a resalable container for up to 3 days.)*

DAIRY-FREE CONDENSED MILK

Substitute this blend cup for cup in any recipe that calls for traditional condensed milk, or use it in Dairy-Free Dulce de Leche (page 209) or Chocolate-Coconut-Oat Magic Bars (page 173).

Makes: **About 1½ cups**   Prep Time: **4 minutes**   Cook Time: **1 hour 30 minutes**

4 cups Homemade Cashew Milk (page 205) or store-bought

1¾ cups sugar

In a small saucepan, bring the milk and sugar to a boil. Reduce the heat and simmer, stirring occasionally to prevent a skin from forming, until reduced by about half and thickened, about 1 hour and 30 minutes. Remove from the heat and cover the surface directly with plastic wrap. Let cool completely. *(The milk will keep refrigerated in a resealable container for up to 2 weeks. If it thickens too much, whisk in some water, 1 teaspoon at a time, to get the desired consistency.)*

DAIRY-FREE WHIPPED CREAM

This luscious whipped cream was a wonderful surprise. After testing many dairy-free milks and thickeners, including cashew milk, almond milk and store-bought coconut creamer, only the cream spooned off the top of a refrigerated can of high-fat coconut milk produced billowy whipped cream. What makes it light and airy is the tiny bit of water whipped in at the end.

Once you've removed the solid cream from the surface of the coconut milk, you will have about ⅔ cup liquid left in the can. I have found that the Thai Kitchen brand of full-fat coconut milk yields the most consistent results. Stick the mixing bowl and electric beaters in the freezer before you start whipping for best results.

Makes: **About 1¼ cups** · Prep Time: **5 minutes**

1 13-ounce can full-fat coconut milk, refrigerated overnight

2 tablespoons confectioners' sugar

⅛ teaspoon salt

1 teaspoon water

Spoon the solid coconut cream from the top of the coconut milk into a medium bowl. With an electric mixer, whip the cream together with the confectioners' sugar on medium-high speed until stiff peaks begin to form. Whip in the salt and water. *(The whipped cream can be refrigerated in a resealable container for up to 1 week.)*

VARIATION

You can make this whipped cream even lighter by whipping in up to ½ cup store-bought marshmallow creme for every 1 cup coconut cream.

DAIRY-FREE DULCE DE LECHE

My recipe for Dairy-Free Condensed Milk makes dulce de leche—caramelized milk—possible. The intensely creamy, caramel spreadable topping is cooked in tight-seal lidded glass jars in the slow cooker. Dulce de leche is perfect spread on toast and topped with some sliced apples or bananas or spooned over dairy-free ice cream or yogurt. Add a sprinkle of cinnamon and you have *cajeta*, a wonderfully comforting Mexican version.

Makes: **About 1¼ cups**   Prep Time: **3 minutes**   Cook Time: **8 hours**

2 cups Dairy-Free Condensed Milk (page 207)

Salt

Combine the condensed milk and a pinch of salt in heatproof glass jars with seal-tight lids and place in a slow cooker. Pour in water to cover the jars by about 1 inch. Cover and cook on low for at least 8 hours or up to 10 hours, depending on your preferred depth of caramelization. Remove the jars and let come to room temperature. *(The dulce de leche can be refrigerated for up to 2 weeks.)*

DAIRY-FREE BÉCHAMEL

The milk-based French white cream sauce called béchamel is pure comfort food, lending body and creamy richness to any dish. Depending on your needs, you can thin it and stir it into soups or use it as a base for macaroni and cheese.

Makes: **About 1½ cups**   Prep Time: **2 minutes**   Cook Time: **12 minutes**

- 2 tablespoons olive oil
- 2 tablespoons My Gluten-Free All-Purpose Flour (page 195)
- 1½ cups Homemade Cashew or Almond Milk (page 205 or 206) or store-bought
- 1 teaspoon salt
- ¼ teaspoon ground nutmeg

In a small saucepan, heat the oil over medium heat. Whisk in the flour and stir until smooth. Slowly whisk in the milk and cook, stirring, until thickened, about 10 minutes. Season with the salt and nutmeg.

VARIATION

DAIRY-FREE GARLIC BÉCHAMEL:
Sauté 2 finely chopped garlic cloves in the olive oil before adding the flour and milk.

DAIRY-FREE SOUR CREAM

The only dairy-free sour creams I've found are made with tofu. I wanted a soy-free alternative, which I achieved with nuts. I've added several layers of acidity, including a dairy-free probiotics powder, to mimic the tartness. You can use this in both sweet and savory recipes, perhaps stirred into a stroganoff or cake batter. The more time you soak the nuts, the smoother the consistency will be.

Makes: **About 1 cup**   Prep Time: **6 minutes (plus soaking)**

1   cup raw cashews, soaked for at least 4 hours or overnight, rinsed and drained

¾   cup water

3   tablespoons lemon juice

1   teaspoon distilled white vinegar

1   teaspoon gluten-free chickpea miso

¾   teaspoon salt

½   teaspoon dairy-free probiotics powder (optional)

Add all the ingredients to a high-speed blender and process on high speed until smooth. Refrigerate until cold and thickened. *(The sour cream keeps in a resealable container for up to 1 week.)*

DAIRY-FREE INSTANT YOGURT

I tasted homemade dairy-free yogurt for the first time at a juice bar in New York City. When I asked the manager what it was made of, I was surprised to learn it was young coconut meat. This recipe is as easy as turning on the blender. The hardest part is tracking down young coconut meat, which comes from a green coconut and is soft and fleshy compared to the solid meat from a mature brown coconut. It can be found in health food shops, Asian stores and online at exoticsuperfoods.com. Vanilla bean seeds add a nice depth of flavor.

If you want to eat the yogurt right away, you can leave out the probiotics. They're great for your digestion, though, and give the yogurt a wonderful tang.

Makes: **About 2 cups**　　Prep Time: **3 minutes**

2 cups young coconut meat

½ cup water

1 tablespoon plus 1 teaspoon agave nectar

Seeds of 1 vanilla bean or 2 teaspoons pure vanilla extract

1 teaspoon dairy-free probiotics powder (optional)

¼ teaspoon salt

Add all the ingredients to a high-speed blender and process on high speed until smooth. Let sit at room temperature until tangy, about 2 hours. Refrigerate until cold. *(The yogurt keeps in a resealable container for up to 1 week.)*

DAIRY-FREE TRADITIONAL YOGURT

I'm addicted to yogurt, and I make this dairy-free version almost every week. Because dairy-free milks tend to have less sugar than cow's milk, adding sugar helps with fermentation by providing food for the bacteria to grow. This low-maintenance yogurt is cultured with a dairy-free starter culture—live, active bacteria. The longer the yogurt ferments, the more sour it will get.

Iota carrageenan, a natural gelling molecule extracted from red algae, produces a soft, almost elastic texture in the yogurt. It's superior to xanthan gum or guar gum for thickening. For best results, use homemade cashew milk, which doesn't have the preservatives or emulsifiers of store-bought brands. You'll also need a simple yogurt maker, which costs about $30.

Makes: **About 4 cups**   Prep Time: **8 minutes**   Cook Time: **20 minutes (plus culturing and chilling)**

4 cups Homemade Cashew Milk (page 205)

2 tablespoons sugar

2¼ teaspoons iota carrageenan

¼ teaspoon dairy-free powdered yogurt starter culture, such as GI ProStart

1. In a medium saucepan, heat the milk and sugar over medium heat, whisking occasionally, until the sugar is dissolved and the temperature measures 110°F on an instant-read thermometer. Add the carrageenan and, using an immersion blender, carefully blend to combine, about 1 minute. Cook over medium-low heat, whisking occasionally, until the carrageenan has dissolved and the temperature reaches 140°F. Remove from the heat. Let cool at room temperature, in the fridge or over an ice bath until the temperature falls to 105°F to 110°F. Add the starter and, using the immersion blender, carefully blend to combine, about 30 seconds. Strain the milk through a fine-mesh sieve.

2. Fill the glass jars of an electric yogurt maker to about 1 inch from the rim. Cap the jars and place in the yogurt maker. Culture the milk, undisturbed, until set and tangy, 5 to 6 hours. Let cool for at least 2 hours to return to room temperature, then refrigerate until completely chilled, about 6 hours or overnight. (*The yogurt will keep for up to 2 weeks.*)

3. To serve, place the yogurt in a medium bowl and blend until creamy with an immersion blender.

VARIATION

DAIRY-FREE GREEK YOGURT: If you prefer thicker yogurt, place the cold yogurt in a cheesecloth–lined strainer set over a bowl, cover with plastic wrap and let drain in the refrigerator until thickened, at least 6 hours.

STIR-INS AND TOPPINGS

STIR-INS

- Maple syrup
- Seeds of 1 vanilla bean or pure vanilla extract
- Chocolate syrup
- Strawberry syrup
- Instant coffee
- Store-bought dairy-free pesto

TOPPINGS

- Wildflower honey and walnuts
- Homemade or store-bought jam
- Stewed figs or prunes
- Maple Nut Granola Clusters (page 14)

DAIRY-FREE RICOTTA CHEESE

Pine nuts lend a nuanced mountain-air flavor to this ricotta stand-in, while macadamia nuts give it extra creaminess. A touch of agave replaces the lactose sugar found in cow's milk.

Makes: **About 2 cups**   Prep Time: **5 minutes (plus soaking)**

- 1 cup raw pine nuts, soaked for at least 4 hours or overnight, rinsed and drained
- 1 cup raw macadamia nuts, soaked for at least 4 hours or overnight, rinsed and drained
- 2 tablespoons olive oil
- 1 tablespoon lemon juice
- 1 teaspoon salt
- ½ teaspoon agave nectar
- ¼ cup plus 1 tablespoon water

Add all the ingredients except the water to a food processor and pulse to combine. With the motor running, slowly stream in the water and process, scraping down the sides of the bowl if necessary, until light and fluffy, about 3 minutes. Refrigerate. *(The ricotta will keep in a resealable container for up to 1 week.)*

VARIATION

For Italian flair, fold in chopped herbs, olives or sun-dried tomatoes after processing.

DAIRY-FREE SWEET RICOTTA CHEESE

I developed this sweet ricotta for desserts like Pumpkin Pie Cannoli with Maple-Candied Pistachios (page 181). I adapted my ricotta cheese recipe (page 215) by substituting neutral-tasting canola oil for the olive oil and adding vanilla extract and orange zest.

Makes: **About 2 cups**   Prep Time: **6 minutes (plus soaking)**

1 cup raw pine nuts, soaked for at least 4 hours or overnight, rinsed and drained

1 cup raw macadamia nuts, soaked for at least 4 hours or overnight, rinsed and drained

3 tablespoons sugar

2 tablespoons lemon juice

2 tablespoons canola oil

1 teaspoon salt

1 teaspoon pure vanilla extract

Zest of 1 orange

¼ cup water

Add all ingredients except the water to a food processor and pulse to combine. With the motor running, slowly stream in the water and process, scraping down the sides of the bowl if necessary, until light and fluffy, about 3 minutes. Refrigerate. *(The ricotta will keep in a resealable container for up to 1 week.)*

VARIATION

Spice things up by adding ¼ teaspoon pumpkin pie spice or ground cinnamon.

DAIRY-FREE GRATED PARMESAN

This speedy recipe gets faux Parmesan cheese on your table in just minutes. I use nutritional yeast, a bright yellow, cheesy-flavored inactive yeast that you can find in your local health food store.

Makes: **About 1 cup**   Prep Time: **1 minute**

¾ cup raw macadamia nuts

¼ cup nutritional yeast

½ teaspoon salt

Using a food processor, pulse together the macadamia nuts, nutritional yeast and salt. Refrigerate. *(The Parmesan will keep in a resealable container for up to 1 week.)*

DAIRY-FREE PARMESAN SHARDS

You'll be amazed at the flavor of this dairy-free Parmesan. It's a pine nut–based cream sauce that's spread into a thin layer and baked at a low temperature until dried. I use agave nectar to round out the flavors, but if you're avoiding or cutting down on sugar, you can leave it out.

Makes: **About 2 cups**   Prep Time: **6 minutes (plus soaking)**   Cook Time: **1 hour 30 minutes**

2 cups raw pine nuts, soaked for at least 4 hours or overnight, rinsed and drained

1 tablespoon lemon juice

2 tablespoons nutritional yeast

2 teaspoons salt

½ cup plus 2 tablespoons water

½ teaspoon agave nectar

1. Preheat the oven to 200°F.
2. Add the pine nuts, lemon juice, nutritional yeast and salt to a food processor and pulse to combine. With the motor running, slowly stream in the water and process, scraping down the sides of the bowl if necessary, until the mixture is smooth and creamy. Stir in the agave.
3. Spread the cream in a thin layer on a parchment paper–lined baking sheet; dehydrate in the oven until completely dried, about 1 hour 30 minutes. Set on a rack to cool completely. Break into pieces. *(The shards can be refrigerated in a resealable container for up to 1 week.)*

DAIRY-FREE GOAT CHEESE

For a flavorful coating, roll the goat cheese in about ⅓ cup toppings such as dried or fresh herbs, chopped nuts, seeds, chopped olives, chopped dried fruit, cracked pepper and spices, or even edible flowers and citrus zest. Using probiotics will give the cheese a nice tang.

Makes: **About 2 cups**   Prep Time: **8 minutes (plus soaking and draining)**

1 cup raw macadamia nuts, soaked for at least 4 hours or overnight, rinsed and drained

1 cup raw cashew nuts, soaked for at least 4 hours or overnight, rinsed and drained

½ cup water

1 teaspoon salt

2 teaspoons lemon juice

1 teaspoon dairy-free probiotics powder (optional)

1. Blend all the ingredients in a high-speed blender until smooth. Place the mixture in a damp cheesecloth-lined strainer set over a bowl and fold the sides of the cheesecloth to loosely cover. Top with a weight and let drain at room temperature for at least 8 hours or up to overnight.

2. To form a log, place the cheese in the middle of a large piece of plastic wrap and roll up, twisting the ends. Refrigerate until set, at least 8 hours, before serving. *(The goat cheese can be refrigerated in a resealable container for up to 1 week.)*

DAIRY-FREE CHEESY FONDUE

This dairy-free knockoff of the classic cheesy dipping sauce will astonish you. The xanthan gum, while optional, gives the fondue its dippable, silky texture, and the miso paste adds a wonderfully fermented, cheese-like flavor. Dip-ables include cubed toasted gluten-free bread, mini hot dogs, French fries, sliced apples, broccoli and celery.

Makes: **About 2 cups**   Prep Time: **8 minutes (plus soaking)**   Cook Time: **10 minutes**

2 cups raw cashew nuts, soaked for at least 4 hours or overnight, rinsed and drained

¾ cup plus 3 tablespoons water

3 tablespoons canola oil

2 garlic cloves, peeled

2 tablespoons nutritional yeast

1 teaspoon gluten-free miso paste

2 teaspoons salt

½ teaspoon xanthan gum (optional)

1 cup dry white wine

1. In a high-speed blender or food processor, blend all the ingredients except the wine, scraping down the sides.

2. Transfer to a medium saucepan, add the wine and cook over medium heat, whisking occasionally, until the alcohol evaporates and the fondue is warmed through, about 10 minutes. Add more water, if necessary, to reach the desired consistency. Serve.

DAIRY-FREE MAYONNAISE

I knew almonds would be the right place to start for this mayo, and I managed to find just the right balance of acidity, saltiness and sweetness. I enjoy this as is and sometimes like to stir in different seasonings like Sriracha, turmeric, relish or smoked chipotle pepper.

Makes: **About 2 cups**   Prep Time: **5 minutes (plus soaking)**

1 cup blanched almonds, soaked for 1 to 2 hours, rinsed and drained

1 cup canola oil

¾ cup water

1 tablespoon distilled white vinegar

2 teaspoons sugar

2 teaspoons salt

Blend all the ingredients in a high-speed blender until smooth. *(The mayonnaise can be refrigerated in a resealable container for up to 1 week.)*

DAIRY-FREE NACHO CHEESE SAUCE

Neutral-flavored cashews are the base for this creamy sauce. Drizzle over corn tortillas, stir into gluten-free macaroni or dip in your favorite crudités. The nutritional yeast contributes a salty cheesiness. For more heat, add a seeded, chopped jalapeño pepper to the blender before processing.

Makes: **About 2 cups**   Prep Time: **8 minutes (plus soaking)**

- 2 cups raw cashew nuts, soaked for at least 4 hours or overnight, rinsed and drained
- ½ cup chopped seeded red bell pepper
- 1 garlic clove, finely chopped
- ½ cup canola oil
- ½ cup water, plus more as needed
- 1 tablespoon lemon juice
- 2 tablespoons nutritional yeast
- 2 teaspoons chili powder or Mexican seasoning
- 2 teaspoons salt
- 1 teaspoon chipotle powder (optional)

Blend all the ingredients together in a high-speed blender or food processor, scraping down the sides, until smooth. Add more water, if necessary, 1 tablespoon at a time, until creamy. *(The sauce can be refrigerated in a resealable container for up to 1 week.)*

DAIRY-FREE RANCH DRESSING

This is my son Isaiah's favorite salad dressing, and I keep it stocked in the fridge to encourage him to eat his greens. If you want to give the dressing more body, blend in xanthan gum, a pinch at a time, until you reach the desired consistency.

Makes: **About 2 cups**   Prep Time: **10 minutes (plus soaking)**

2 cups raw cashews, soaked for at least 4 hours or overnight, rinsed and drained

1 cup water

¼ cup canola oil

¼ cup white wine vinegar

2 teaspoons dried herb blend, such as Italian

1 tablespoon garlic salt

1 teaspoon onion powder

½ teaspoon black pepper

1 teaspoon honey

Blend all the ingredients in a high-speed blender until smooth. Transfer to a bowl and refrigerate until cold. *(The dressing will keep in a resealable container for up to 1 week.)*

ACKNOWLEDGMENTS

I would not exist without the unconditional love I receive daily from my beautiful, miraculous children, Isaiah and Chiara. They truly are my greatest accomplishments. They are the light that guides me in and out of the kitchen. I can only hope that I give them the same.

To my mother, Penny, my father, Silverio, and my brother, Bernardo—all of you have been my huge support. An extra hug and kiss to my mom, who relentlessly walked alongside me through the development of this entire cookbook—from reviewing recipe ideas to taste-testing desserts to reading the final pages. She was, and always will be, an endless source of love, truth and encouragement.

To my handsome Billy Ticali, you're the truest embodiment of "everything happens for a reason." I was lucky that you came into my life just when you were supposed to and brought me the love, positive energy and laughter I craved.

To my closest lifelong friend, Allyson Fisher, your patience and kindness are irreplaceable. And to my dear friends Jennifer Perillo, Zoe Pellegrino, Brittany Angell and Sasha Sekinger your generosity is immeasurable.

To my longtime agent, Doe Coover, who continues to surprise and delight me with her ideas and support, both professionally and personally. To my editor, Rux Martin, who pushes me beyond my comfort zone and pulls words out of me. She has inspired me to be a better writer.

To my friend and the most talented photographer I've ever met, John Kernick. It's hard to believe we've known each other for nearly two decades. He captures the moment, and everyone can't help but fall in love with each and every photograph.

To my dear friend Tracey Seaman, who has kept me happily fed since the day I met her at *Food & Wine* right after I graduated from college. I trust everything she says and does. She is the best food stylist I could have. To my recipe testers, Amy Howard Williams and Emiko Shimojo, who worked tirelessly to make sure every recipe would work for everyone. To the rest of my photography crew—Maysoon Faraj, Brooke Deonarine, Rizwan Alvi, Christina Stanley-Salerno—these guys always make me look and feel so good.

To all of you who believe in me—and my recipes—I wouldn't be here without you. Thank you for trusting me to help you and your families through often-challenging times on our journey together toward happily living gluten free and dairy free.

INDEX